HANDMADE
CHIC

*Fashionable Projects
That Look High-End,
Not Homespun*

LAURA BENNETT
NEW YORK

RODALE.

Mention of specific companies, organizations, or authorities in this book does not imply endorsement by the author or publisher, nor does mention of specific companies, organizations, or authorities imply that they endorse this book, its author, or the publisher. Internet addresses and telephone numbers given in this book were accurate at the time it went to press.

© 2012 by Laura Bennett
Illustrations © 2012 by Laura Bennett
Photographs © 2012 by Edward Smith

Rodale books may be purchased for business or promotional use or for special sales. For information, please write to:
Special Markets Department, Rodale, Inc., 733 Third Avenue, New York, NY 10017

Printed in the United States of America
Rodale Inc. makes every effort to use acid-free ♾, recycled paper ♻.

Book design by Kara Plikaitis

Library of Congress Cataloging-in-Publication Data

Bennett, Laura.
    Handmade chic : fashionable projects that look high-end, not homespun / Laura Bennett.
       p.   cm.
    Includes index.
    ISBN 978–1–60961–300–6 hardcover
    1. Dress accessories.   2. Leatherwork.   I. Title.
    TT649.8.B46 2011
    646.4'8—dc23
                                                2011030332

Distributed to the trade by Macmillan

2 4 6 8 10 9 7 5 3 1 hardcover

We inspire and enable people to improve their lives and the world around them.
www.rodalebooks.com

To Peter, my greatest supporter and biggest fan.

SMALL LUXURIES 22

section I

FASHIONABLY ORGANIZED 60

section II

Contents

STYLISH CARRYALLS 110

section III

EVENING EXTRAVAGANCES 160

section IV

INTRODUCTION

My children occasionally lift their faces from the computer screen long enough to ask me what I did as a child, curious to know how I survived before YouTube. I assure them that not only had man invented the wheel, but that he had also created three network TV channels, and when I wasn't pretending to be Ginger from Gilligan's Island, I did crafts. For my 10th birthday, my mother gave me a sewing machine—most likely to keep me from breaking hers. Sewing opened up a whole new world for me, and I left egg carton caterpillars and tissue paper flowers behind. I started sewing pillows and tote bags, and eventually moved on to Kwik Sew and Sew EZ types of patterns, apparently unbothered by their alternative spellings. By 13 years old, I had started getting creative with the patterns—adding the top of this one to the bottom of that one—and before too long I'd started making patterns of my own. Patterns for beginning sewers are still available, and I recommend learning to sew by getting a simple pattern from your local sewing store and following the step-by step directions.

Because I had sewn for so much of my life, I was unaware that not everyone was out there throwing together evening gowns with a couple of yards of fabric and some well-selected trim. When I became a contestant on season three of Bravo's fashion design reality series Project Runway, I started to understand that the creative process fascinates people. As complicated as they may look, the items that I made on Project Runway and continue to make today are actually quite simple: I'm really still in the Very Easy Vogue state of mind. How else could I have pulled off design challenges such as "Create a gown for the Miss Universe Pageant—in 3 hours and with $30—with materials from a hardware store"? I know how to be quick and crafty, to say the least. I've never been to fashion school or had more than the most basic sewing lesson from my mom. Every project in this book is certainly simple enough for anyone who can thread a needle and sew a straight seam, and some projects don't even require any sewing.

EVERY PROJECT IN THIS BOOK IS CERTAINLY SIMPLE ENOUGH FOR ANYONE WHO CAN THREAD A NEEDLE AND SEW A STRAIGHT SEAM.

That said, this book is different from most of the sewing project books I've seen (and bought) in recent years. While those tend to have a crafty, country, quaint sensibility, I like to think that my projects (and their endless possible variations) are upscale, chic, and urbane. They reflect the glamorous look and feel that I became known for during my time on Project Runway and that got me all the way to New York Fashion Week. No small feat for an untrained home sewer.

Some of the projects in this book are accessory items sewn from scratch. Some are embellishment techniques that you can use on a garment you sew, buy at a store, or already have hanging in your closet. Other projects are about transforming something out of date or out of use into something new and exciting. Be warned that this is not Dressmaking 101: There are no instructions for how to create a skirt by sewing a triangle of fabric to a pair of jeans or fashion a purse out of a cigar box. In this book, I offer a thoroughly modern approach to DIY.

The projects in this book are organized in skill-building order, from easiest to most difficult, and are laid out in simple steps. Every material or technique I suggest throughout is explained in either Materials and Techniques (see page 2) or Sewing (see page 17), so take the time to read these sections before getting started on the projects and refer back as you encounter new materials and procedures. When you're ready to begin, I recommend getting your feet wet with some of the smaller projects and then moving on to the larger ones. None of them is difficult when done step by step, but if you try out a few projects from Small Luxuries (see page 22), you'll become familiar working with materials that may be new to you, such as leather or feathers, and you'll find that the same techniques and design elements are used in more complex projects later on. Once you've successfully completed a few projects, you'll be amazed by how talented you really are.

Along with step-by-step instructions and illustrations, I've also included patterns and templates throughout, as well as a list of resources (see page 199). I've been mindful of the fact that most of you don't live a short distance from New York City's garment district, so I've made sure

THE PROJECTS IN THIS BOOK ARE ORGANIZED IN SKILL-BUILDING ORDER, FROM EASIEST TO MOST DIFFICULT, AND ARE LAID OUT IN SIMPLE STEPS.

that every item I use in this book, down to the smallest bead, is available online. I've also included the names of my favorite stores here in New York, so you can place an order by phone or just come by and find me wandering the aisles.

Whatever project you choose to make, I highly recommend using quality materials. The old adage about buying the best you can afford holds true here. I prefer the feel of real, soft, buttery leather in my hands, and I'm sure you will, too. Plastic beads will never shine the way real crystal beads do, so invest in the good stuff, and be sure to buy the best quality thread because it is no fun to work with cheap thread that tangles and breaks. You will spend a little more, but your projects will be more enjoyable to work on and they'll last longer, too. And just think of all the money you'll be saving by doing the handwork yourself. (I'm good at rationalizations; I have a closet full of pricey shoes because I save so much money sewing my own clothes.)

Have you ever wondered why high-end luxury items cost as much as they do? The answer is craftsmanship. A top-end handbag may take a craftsman as much as 40 hours to sew by hand. Quality is also a factor in price. Only the finest, most unblemished skins make the grade.

Finally, luxury items are products of exquisite design. You have probably noticed as you look through the accessories section of your local department store that the simple things are always the most difficult to find. That's because they are the most difficult to produce well. When there are no superfluous zippers, flaps, or pockets to hide bad construction, every flaw shows. Cheap leather has no place to hide. In a well-designed item, every element has a function and a purpose. It's the simple black dress that has to be cut just right from the best-quality fabric—and that's the dress we all need.

Maybe one day you will be able to walk into a fine leather goods store and treat yourself to whatever you want, or maybe you already can. But if you want to make the most out of the projects in this book and achieve that high-end look at home, I encourage you to think of yourself as a craftsman, use quality materials, take your time, and be precise.

As simple and straightforward as these projects are, the results are truly spectacular. When people catch a glimpse of your finished pieces, they won't ask, "Did you make that?" They'll ask, "Where did you get that?" or "What designer is that?" Your friends will barely believe you when you say, "I made it myself."

INSPIRATION . . .

. . . TO ACCESSORIZE

Materials and Techniques
Working with Leather

I AM ENAMORED OF THE feel, the smell, the colors, and the textures of leather. I'm not sure if I love bags and shoes because they are made of leather or if I love leather because it is what bags and shoes are made of. It's my personal chicken/egg dilemma. If you've never worked with leather before, don't be intimidated. Working with leather is a lot like working with fabric—and well-behaved, forgiving fabric, at that. It comes in an endless array of colors and textures, and it has great body and just enough stretch so you can fudge. Plus, the edges don't unravel.

Purchasing Leather

Leather is priced by the square foot but sold by the hide or side (half a hide), which, because it depends on the animal it came from, can vary greatly in size. A cowhide may be 40 square feet, while a lamb or goat hide is only 6 or 8 square feet. If you are not ready for an entire hide, don't worry. I've never been in a leather store that didn't have a remnant bin, which is a great place to look for pieces for smaller projects. (Just be sure to bring your project pattern with you so you purchase enough leather.) Also, you can always ask if a hide can be cut. Another great source for smaller pieces of leather is eBay. Search for "leather square feet," and hundreds of pieces of various sizes will show up.

Leather's thickness is referred to in ounces. A thin 1-ounce leather, such as lambskin or calfskin, is no thicker than a medium-weight fabric such as twill or gabardine. I use this weight for linings. A 2-ounce leather, like calfskin or goatskin, is perfect for small items, like the Eyeglasses Case or Zipper Pouch projects in Section I: Small Luxuries. Thicker leather (3 ounces and up), such as cowhide, is best used for the outsides of bags, but anything thicker than 4 or 5 ounces would be difficult to sew with an ordinary sewing machine. Try to choose soft rather than stiff leather whenever possible; the stitches tend to sink into the softer leather and look neater.

Leather comes in an endless variety of colors and textures. A favorite of mine is cow leather embossed to look like exotic animal skins such as lizard, ostrich, alligator, or crocodile. Rarely do I say that the imitation of anything is better than the original, but this is an exception. I do love the look of real alligator and crocodile, but the problem—in addition to the exorbitant expense—is that the belly is the only piece of prime real estate; the rest of the skin is too tough and scaly. It can take four bellies to make a single crocodile bag. Embossed cow leather, on the other hand, comes in large pieces with a pattern that repeats itself over and over, giving you many bellies for multiple projects. So unless you have an alligator farm in your backyard (and believe it or not, having grown up in Louisiana I know someone who does), I highly recommend using the embossed leather to add instant detail and textural interest to your projects.

Sewing with Leather

The first question I am asked when someone finds out that I make my own leather accessories is, "Do you sew them on a regular sewing machine?" The answer is yes, with two simple modifications. First, you should replace your machine's regular fabric needle with a leather needle in size 14 or 16. Leather needles are available where sewing notions are sold and have a blade-shaped end that helps cut into the leather as it moves through the machine. Second, you should use a heavy-duty or denim-weight thread, which is slightly

heavier than all-purpose thread and emulates the look of high-end, hand-sewn leather goods. If you don't have heavy-duty or denim-weight thread, a good-quality all-purpose thread will work just fine.

My leather-sewing machine of choice is an old Singer model 66 that I bought on eBay. These old machines are widely available and cost anywhere from $40 (including shipping) to $400, depending on the mental status of the seller, so watch for bargains and don't feel like you have to buy the first model you see listed. Other models to look for are the Singer 99 and 15-91: These are straight-stitch only machines that were manufactured from 1920 through the 1950s with few or no modifications. If you already have a machine that can sew denim, you may not even need to purchase a new one to make these projects. Try sewing leather with your machine, and if the stitching comes out looking good on the top but not on the bottom, just increase the tension. I generally use a contrasting color thread when I sew, but if you don't trust your skills or your machine isn't quite as happy as mine is when presented with leather, I suggest you match your thread color to your leather color. This strategy will hide a multitude of sins. But don't worry: With just a bit of trial and error you will quickly get a sense of what leathers you—and your sewing machine—are comfortable working with.

Leather Adhesives

There are many types of leather adhesive on the market, but I find that tape gives me the most control, without the noxious fumes and wait times of contact cements or the messiness of spray adhesives. The kind I prefer and recommend for every leather project in this book is 3M 465 Adhesive Transfer Tape. It's a thin adhesive on a paper tape (similar to double stick tape) that you apply to the back of your leather, burnish, and then peel the paper away from. It comes in various widths, from $\frac{1}{8}$ inch to 12 inches wide, but I find the 1-inch-wide roll to be the most useful because the size suits a variety of purposes. I can lay several strips next to each other to cover a large piece of leather, or I can cut it into thin strips to apply it to small areas. Because this tape is an industrial product, it is usually sold by the case; however, you can buy single rolls online or at an art supply store (see Resources on page 199). I recently bought a pair of nonstick scissors at Staples, and while they are certainly not a necessity, I highly recommend them for cutting the adhesive tape. (My husband likes to point out that I have nonstick scissors in my toolbox but I have no nonstick pans in my kitchen.)

Cutting Leather

I don't usually cut my leather with scissors because I find that I get more precise, accurate cuts with a razor. I use snap blade cutters, also known as box cutters, because I like the convenience of snapping off an old blade and having a sharp, fresh one appear without my having to go looking for replacement blades. I also like the retractable feature because it means I'll never look up to find my 3-year-old armed with a razor blade. If you prefer to use fabric shears, a nice, sharp pair will also work well for cutting leather (or fabric, of course). Just don't ever use them to cut paper—not even pattern paper—and certainly not tape, because they will become dull. And hide them from your kids, or they'll quickly ruin them by using them to cut construction paper.

For a cutting surface, I recommend using a self-healing cutting mat, available at any art supply store. Not only do these mats extend the life of your cutting blades, they also have a printed grid that helps you mark and measure leather or pattern pieces. I also suggest you invest in a leather hole punch to create clean openings for installing hardware. The ice pick in your kitchen drawer will not remove the leather as effectively as an actual hole punch will. Leather hole punches have a rotating dial with a variety of sizes, and they're readily available at hardware stores.

Finishing Leather

Leather products require some finishing on the edges to look professional. Leather supply Web sites sell a product called gum tragacanth: a clear, viscous liquid that helps to compress the fibers and keep the edges of the leather from becoming fuzzy. When a piece is finished, simply apply the gum tragacanth to the edges with your finger and rub it in using the back of a spoon or a similar smooth object. The leather edges may darken, but once the gum tragacanth dries they will return to their original color. This product is available through any leather craft supplier and is often just referred to as "gum."

Due to the effects of finishes and dyes, the cut edge of leather is occasionally a dramatically different color than the leather's surface. If the effect is unattractive, simply mix a bit of acrylic paint to match the surface color and apply it to the edges with a cotton swab or small paintbrush. Keep a damp paper towel on hand to immediately wipe away any paint that wanders off the edge and gets on the leather's surface. (This has to be done before the paint has a chance to dry.) If you will be topstitching your project in a contrasting thread color, be sure to paint before topstitching. This will let you avoid painting the stitching that's close to the edge.

Alternate Materials

Any of the leather projects in this book can also be made with fabrics such as denim, canvas, corduroy, or felt. When working with one of these materials, I recommend cutting out the pattern pieces on the true bias, at a 45-degree angle to the fabric's grain. This will allow you to leave the edges raw, and the bias cut to produce a controlled, frayed edge. (Note that felt has no grain and can be cut in any direction.) I also find that sometimes I need to add additional layers of fabric to straps in order to accommodate hardware that requires a certain thickness. To do this, I

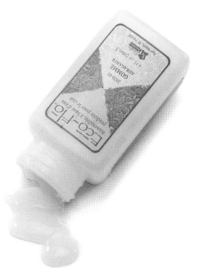

use the same adhesive transfer tape that I use to adhere leather. If you use fabric in the projects that follow, where the instructions call for two layers of leather for a strap, you may want to cut three or four layers of fabric and adhere them together with the tape. Another great mterial that can be used for any project in this book is Ultrasuede. It is a man-made synthetic suede that comes in several weights and a wide array of colors.

Leather Hardware

Adding hardware to your leather pieces is like adding jewelry to an outfit: It can set the tone to casual, fancy, or professional. Most of the hardware in this book cannot be found in craft stores across the country (which I think adds to its allure), but my favorite hardware source, www.hardwareelf.com, has it all available on its Web site for quick and easy purchase.

Each set of hardware is applied a little bit differently, and hardware does not generally come with manufacturer's directions. Luckily, though, all of the components you need are sold together as a group. You will install some hardware by simply cutting slots and inserting and bending prongs. Some pieces will have backplates that are held in place with small screws, and some require the leather to be cut away or hole-punched for the parts to work properly. Each of my projects that requires hardware has detailed instructions on how to install that particular kind, and if you choose a different style, most have a similar method with just minor variations.

The only tools you will need to install most hardware are a small flathead screwdriver or a small Phillips head screwdriver, a leather hole punch, and your trusty snap blade cutter, cutting mat, and straight edge. I provide templates for the installations that require the leather to be cut away, but you can always mark any spots you need to cut by applying chalk to the back of the hardware, pressing it in place, and then using the chalk marks to form the cutouts.

Getting to the point in a project where it is time to attach the hardware is always exciting. With just a few cuts and turns of a screw, you get to take your handiwork to a whole new level.

WORKING WITH FUR

LET'S JUST GET THE CONTROVERSIAL subject of fur over with. Some people don't wear fur for ethical reasons. I have total respect for those who choose to live a vegan lifestyle and not partake of animal products of any kind, and I'm perfectly willing to discuss the pros and cons with them (though I doubt anyone will be able to talk me out of leather and fur and into vegan footwear). I once had a woman lean over from the next table in a restaurant and berate me for wearing fur. She was having steak for lunch. I didn't feel compelled to engage in a conversation with her about the evils of the fur industry.

While I don't have an ethical problem with fur, I do find that most furs are difficult to wear. They often look dated, are visually heavy, and make the wearer look old. (Nothing says middle-aged mafia wife like a full-length mink coat.) There are some designers who work with fur in a fresh and modern way, but their pieces tend to be very expensive, even by fur standards. By taking apart vintage furs and remaking them into something updated, as I do in the projects in this book, you not only save money, but you also save a castaway item that would otherwise have gone unused.

Buying Vintage Fur

I buy most of my vintage furs from eBay, and I usually get stoles because they are the least expensive and most readily available. Vintage fur coats, jackets, wraps, and stoles are also available at antique marts, thrift stores, and vintage clothing stores. Old furs can be too fragile to work with if the skin is dried out. You can always check a fur for dryness by giving a gentle tug to see if the skin splits. When I am purchasing a fur over the Internet, I always ask the seller if the fur is dried out. They sometimes arrive dried out anyway, but at least I feel I have a right to return them if I asked the question first. Another tip for purchasing furs from eBay is to add the words "craft" or "cutter" to your search. These terms will bring up damaged furs that are no longer fit to wear but are perfect for taking apart and using to make accessories. I also find that once your friends know that you are looking for vintage fur pieces, they magically start appearing. It seems that a lot of people have a forgotten granny fur in the back of their closet just waiting to be turned into something modern.

Sewing Fur

Sewing fur requires no special sewing skills or tools. The leather that the fur is attached to is quite thin and can easily be sewn on a home sewing machine using common size 10 or 12 needles and all-purpose thread. You may sew seams using a zigzag or a straight stitch, and I recommend tucking in the hairs as you sew. Any hairs that are caught in the seam allowance can be picked out later using a straight pin.

Cutting Fur

Cutting fur is different from cutting fabric. You want to be sure to cut through the leather only, not the hairs, or your seams will look bald. I always cut from the leather side with a snap blade cutter, pressing just hard enough to cut the leather without cutting the hairs on the other side. You can also use scissors. From the leather side, run the bottom blade of the scissors along the leather to part the fur, making small clips as you go.

Before you start working on any vintage fur, I recommend removing the existing lining and interfacing by using a small pair of scissors or a seam ripper to clip the threads holding them in place. This eliminates unnecessary bulk and makes it possible to trace a pattern piece on the skin side of the fur. Once you get down to the actual skins, you'll be amazed by the amount of workmanship involved in piecing a fur garment.

Faux Fur

If real fur is not your thing, any of these projects can be made with faux fur. There are some amazing faux furs available in fabric stores, but all are not created equal. I find that the most realistic-looking brand is Tissavel. Its faux fur comes in a variety of colors and styles; my favorite is the faux white mink. However, if obviously fake and fun is the look you are going for, fabric stores carry a wide variety of crazy colors and textures, too. Cut fake fur the same way you would real fur: from the back, with a snap blade cutter (to avoid cutting the hairs).

WORKING WITH BEADS

I LOVE BEADING ON A dress. Just flash something sparkly in front of me and I'll bite like a fish every time. If you would like to really stand out at your next formal event, consider adding beads to your clothing or accessories. Even the most mundane, off-the-rack garment turns into something stunning when a beautiful splash of colorful beads is added to a neckline, hem, or waistband. Beads add a sparkle and richness that is sure to get you noticed when you enter a room.

The beading projects in this book use a technique I came up with when I was making my final collection for *Project Runway.* Faced with having to put together a collection for New York Fashion Week in only 2 months, I needed to add a "wow" factor to garments without taking the time to intricately bead an entire dress. People still stop me on the street because they remember a particular dress from that collection that featured a beading pattern that appeared to fade away. This dress had an unusual color combination of gray and chartreuse and was the highlight of my finale collection.

Keep in mind that I use the term "beading" loosely. By beading, I mean applying beads, sequins, and especially some faux gems called hot-fix rhinestones. Personally, I think the invention of hot-fix rhinestones is right up there with penicillin. Adhesive is pre-applied to the back of the stones, so you just need an everyday home iron to apply them—no messy glues required. Hot-fix rhinestones come in several sizes, from the smallest—SS10 (2.8 mm) to the largest—SS34 (7.3 mm). I tend to use several sizes mixed together in a project. The stones are sold in packages by the dozen, the gross, or in envelopes of 10 gross. They're available in an amazing array of colors, and I often use several shades of the same color family together. For example, if I am using three sizes for a project, I will purchase the stones in rose, pink, and fuchsia. As you'll see later on, you can use hot-fix rhinestones on clothing, bags, or shoes.

Applying Hot-Fix Rhinestones

To apply the rhinestones, simply place your item to be embellished on an ironing board or other flat surface and arrange your stones as you would like them to appear. To place your stones, I recommend using what I call the "scatter and turn" method: Sprinkle the stones in an area, hope that at least 50 percent fall with the adhesive side down, and then turn the stones that don't.

Next, place an iron set to the wool setting (no steam) on top of the stones for 7 to 15 seconds. (Use less time for the smaller stones than for the larger stones.) Just reposition your iron until all of the stones in one section are set, then move on to a new section.

When I am working on an item that can't lie flat on an ironing board, such as shoes, I use a handheld tool called a hot fixer to apply the stones. You simply plug in this device, let it heat up, and place the tip over each rhinestone for the necessary amount of time. The process is a bit more tedious than ironing on a bunch of rhinestones all at once, but sometimes it is the only way to get sparkle in hard-to-reach places.

Hot-fix rhinestones are so easy to use that you simply can't make a mistake. The hardest part of using them is deciding where on a garment to add dazzling sparkle. Be warned: These rhinestones are addicting and you may find yourself embellishing the hand towels in your bathroom.

Sewing Beads

When embellishing a garment with hot-fix rhinestones, I often add a few regular beads as a focal point, for texture, or as an accent. Simple beading requires only a needle, thread, and beads. Be sure to choose a needle small enough to pass through the hole in the bead you've chosen. I generally prefer to match the thread to the background fabric color (as opposed to the bead color) for two reasons: It makes the stitch appear to sink into the background, and you won't have to constantly switch thread colors if you have many different colors of beads.

To sew beads onto a garment, begin by threading your needle and knotting one end of the thread. Bring the needle up through the fabric to the right side of the garment and thread a bead onto the needle. Do a backstitch by bringing the needle back through the fabric behind the bead. Sew through each bead twice to secure it and to help prevent it from flopping around. Get to the spot for your next bead by sewing small stitches along the way. (If your thread matches your fabric, these stitches will not show.) Be careful never to pull the thread so tight that it puckers your fabric.

WORKING WITH FEATHERS

A GIRL CAN REALLY WEAR only so many beaded dresses, so I went looking for another form of glam to spruce up the simple silhouettes I prefer to wear. That's when I discovered feathers. Floating and fabulous, feathers add incredible movement to a garment. The method shown in this book to add feathers to garments and accessories surely isn't one I invented, but it served me well when I used it in my *Project Runway* finale collection at New York Fashion Week.

The tricks to working with feathers are in the dyeing and the tying. I most often use ostrich feathers, which come as a trim that can be purchased by the yard. These trims are usually bound with a bulky fabric tape and can't be sewn onto the surface of the garment, so I use a tying technique that is not very different from tying fly-fishing lures. You may even be able to talk your husband into sitting down and bundling the feathers for you. Think of it as kind of a fashion/fishing/bonding experience.

Dyeing Feathers

Dyeing is important because most feathers come in colors appropriate for ballroom dancing costumes and tend to be overly bright and gaudy. Because a feather-trimmed dress is already over the top, you certainly want the color to be tasteful. Dyeing the feathers yourself gives you endless options for matching or contrasting with your chosen fabrics. You will also end up with more sophisticated shades due to the slight color variations that are a byproduct of the dyeing process. I recommend starting with off-white or white feathers when custom dyeing. I once made a dress that graduated from dark to pale yellow for a fashion show honoring Charles Schulz, the creator of the Peanuts characters. I thought it was the best Woodstock-inspired dress in the entire show. (My Pigpen dress in a cloud of brown tulle was also pretty impressive.)

To dye ostrich feather trim, dissolve ¼ cup of liquid Rit Dye in 4 cups of very hot water in a glass bowl. (I heat the water in a teapot until just before it comes to a boil.) Submerge your feather trim entirely in the dye and let it soak until it looks darker than you'd like the final color to turn out; this will probably take between 2 and 5 minutes. (When the feathers dry, they will be lighter in color than they appear when wet.) Once you've achieved the right color, take the feather trim out of the dye and spread it out on a paper towel to soak up the excess dye.

To dye feathers in a series of progressively lighter shades, start with a full-strength formula, dissolving ¼ cup of liquid Rit Dye in 4 cups of water. Once the darkest shade of feathers has been dyed, pour out half of the dye solution and replace that half with water. After dyeing the next set of feathers, again pour out half of the dye and replace it with water. As the solution becomes more and more diluted, the feathers will come out lighter.

To return the feathers to their original fluffiness, blow-dry the trim with a hair drier set on the coolest setting. It may take a while, but I promise that just when you think your trim is never going to look like anything but a drowned chicken, the feathers will magically fluff up. Once they are dry, they are ready to be cut and tied.

Tying Feathers

Start with a piece of dyed ostrich trim long enough to cover the section you want to feather. (Each project's directions will specify the amount needed.) Cut a 12-inch piece of thread for each bundle of feathers that you'll make for your project. Cut ½ inch of the feathers from the trim where the feathers meet the fabric tape. (1) This will make a bundle of approximately 15 individual feathers, but close counts here, so don't make yourself crazy trying for bundles of exactly 15 feathers. Pinch the cut feathers together at the top and hold them between your thumb and forefinger about ½ inch from the cut end. Hold one 12-inch piece of thread under your thumb ½ inch from the end, leaving a 2-inch tail. (2) With your free hand, begin tightly winding the thread up to the end of the feather bundle (3) and back down to your thumb, so that the long thread tail ends up near the 2-inch thread tail. (4) Knot the two tails together. (5) Trim the short tail, but leave the long tail to be used to sew the bundle onto your creation. (6)

These feather projects are time-consuming, so I suggest that you get your materials together and sit down in front of a *House* marathon on TV. Or a *Real Housewives* marathon. I'm not judging.

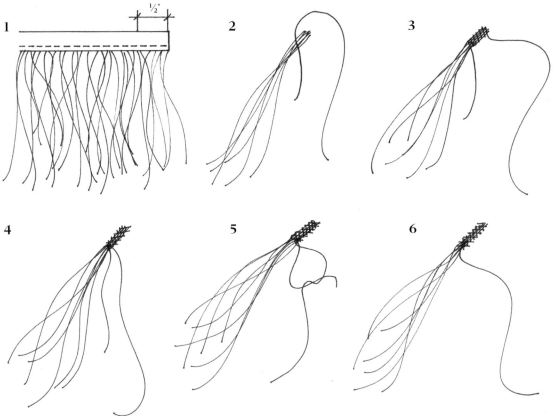

SEWING

SEWING IS A LOT LIKE COOKING: You can have drawers full of exotic gadgets and an extensive knowledge of advanced techniques, but there are actually only a few essential tools and skills you need in order to get the job done. Here is a short list of the sewing tools and terminology you'll need to have and know to get you through this book.

Sewing Tools

Sewing Machine. Sewing machines range from simple, old-fashioned, hand-crank models to modern, complex, computerized devices—and you can find everything in between, too. If you don't sew often or are getting used to a new machine, don't be overwhelmed by its features; there are just a few things you really need to know. First of all, learn to thread your machine exactly the way the manufacturer recommends. This is a time when close does not count: Every step must be done in the proper order. If you start to sew and your stiches look wrong, either on the top or the bottom, I can almost guarantee that your machine is not threaded properly. Don't go diving for the tension knob; machine tensions are set by the manufacturers and rarely need major adjusting. Only the slightest tension adjustment should be necessary. Again, if your stitches are coming out funky, it is more likely that you have a threading problem.

Next, you need to know how to wind and replace your machine's bobbin. You should also be able to remove the needle and replace it, being careful to do so in the right direction. Finally, you must learn to adjust your stitch length and sew forward and in reverse. If you no longer have the manual that came with your machine, or if you never had it, search for it online. Most companies now have their manuals available on the Web, and it is worth the time to print one out and keep it near your sewing machine.

Thread. All-purpose thread will work for most of the projects here, but I do use a heavy-duty thread on leather because I prefer the look. In sewing stores, heavy-weight threads are called upholstery thread, denim thread, heavy-duty thread, or T-40. Color options are usually more limited in these types of threads, however, so if you would like to

match your thread exactly to your leather or fabric, all-purpose thread may be what you need.

Sewing Machine Needles. Sewing machine needles are sold in packs of all the same size or in packs of assorted sizes, and they're numbered. Smaller numbers mean finer needles. Regular size 10 or 12 needles, known as sharps, are fine for sewing anything in this book but leather. You will see size 14 or 16 leather sewing needles listed in the Tools for every project that involves sewing leather.

Hand-Sewing Needles. Hand sewing needles are also numbered, but in this case the larger the number, the finer the needle. (They just couldn't make it easy!) You don't need to worry about the size of a hand-sewing needle as much as you do a sewing machine needle. In fact, I have never known the number of any hand-sewing needle I have ever used—I usually just dig out one that looks to be the right size. (My kids like to push them way into my pincushion.)

Pins and Pincushion. Taking the time to pin fur and fabric pieces together before you sew them saves trouble in the end. The type of pin you use is up to you. I prefer long, heavy pins, which tend to be dull, but some may prefer the small, sharp ones. Whichever type you choose, I do recommend pinning your pieces together by inserting the pins perpendicular to the seam to be sewn, with the head of the pin hanging off the fabric. This allows you to pull out the pin regardless of the direction you sew in. I also recommend that you keep a pincushion close by so your pins don't end up on the floor. (My dog likes to eat them, so I try to save him the pain and us the vet bills by putting them directly in the pincushion once they're out of the fabric.) When it comes to leather, you may use small binder clips to hold pieces together.

Fine-point Permanent Marker or Tailor's Chalk. These marking utensils allow you to draft or trace pattern pieces directly onto your fabric. I use a fine-point permanent marker on leather, always on the wrong side, and chalk on fabric because you can dust it away when you're finished with it. Tracing a pattern piece onto fabric or leather and then cutting it out will give you more accurate results than you'll get by trying to cut around a pattern piece that has been pinned in place.

Sewing Terminology

Right and Wrong Side. The side of the fabric or leather that ends up on the outside of your project is called the right side. Conversely, the side that ends up on the inside is called the wrong side. You can choose whichever side you want to have face out—it doesn't have to be the manufacturer's idea of the right side. For instance, you may prefer the sueded side of the leather or the lighter side of the fabric to be on the outside. Just be consistent when you're cutting out the pattern pieces.

Cutting on the Bias. Woven fabrics have threads running in two directions, forming a grid. This is called the fabric's grain. Cutting on the bias means that your pattern pieces are cut at a 45-degree angle to the grain of the fabric. When you cut a woven fabric on the bias, the pieces will have some stretch and the edges will fray in a controlled manner. Bias-cut fabric can be used as an alternative to any leather project.

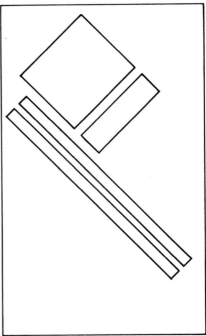

Back-Tacking. Back-tacking a sewn seam adds strength to a point of stress. To back-tack, simply reverse the sewing direction of your machine and re-sew over the previous three or four stitches.

Running Stitch. This is the stitch most common to hand sewing. You will use it in this book to baste a seam (add a temporary row of stitching that will be removed) and to gather fabric. Using a threaded needle with a knot at the end, insert the needle down into the fabric on the right side and bring it back up through the fabric from the wrong side at evenly spaced intervals.

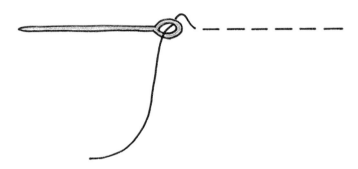

Slip Stitch. This is a perfect stitch to close openings left for turning pieces inside out. Fasten a knotted thread at one end of the opening to be sewn closed. Bring the needle and thread out to the top on one side. For the first and each succeeding stitch, slip the needle down through the bottom side, and up through the opposite edge. Bring the needle out and draw the thread through. Continue to slip the needle and thread through the opposing edges until the opening is fully closed.

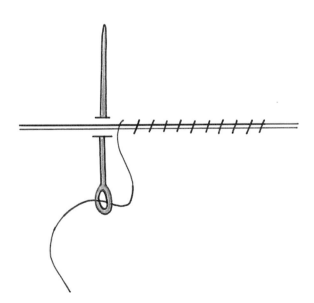

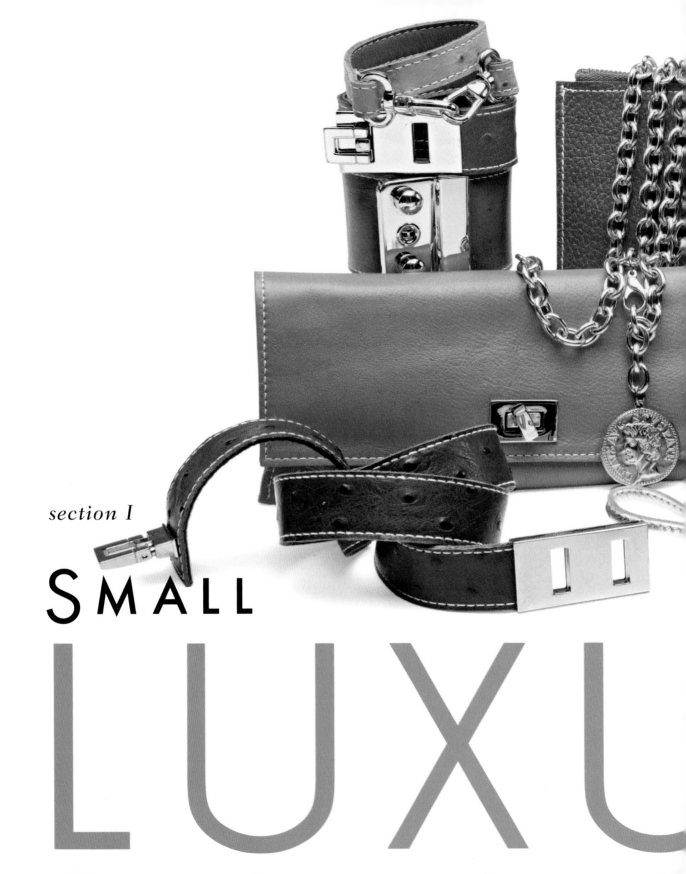

SMALL
LUXU

URIES

In the movie *Steel Magnolias*, actress Olympia Dukakis declares, "The only thing that separates us from the animals is our ability to accessorize." I'm not sure that accessories are the best gauge of evolutionary advancement, but they definitely bring out the differences between one person and another. You can give the same simple dress to five women and I assure you, once they add accessories, their looks will be totally different. The projects in this section give you the opportunity to personalize your most essential, everyday garments. Many of them are small enough to be made from a leather or heavy-weight fabric item you already have, so think about recycling an old bag or belt.

The projects in this section are small and easy to manage, but the cutting, sewing, adhering, and hardware installation required for them are the basic skills and techniques needed to complete even the most complex projects in the book. You will see that these simple forms and techniques become the basis for more advanced designs. For tips, tricks, and general questions about creating leather accessories, refer to Working with Leather on page 2.

BUSINESS CARD HOLDER

Make an impression in the business world with this simple but elegant business card holder. This straightforward project will help you become familiar with cutting and sewing leather. Use a piece of leather with a bit of body—something with the stiffness of cereal box–weight cardboard—for professional-looking results.

MATERIALS

½ square foot 3-ounce leather
3M 465 adhesive transfer tape
Gum tragacanth or acrylic paint
Heavy-duty or all-purpose thread

TOOLS

Sewing machine
Size 14 or 16 leather sewing machine needles
Snap blade cutter
Self-healing cutting mat
Metal straight edge

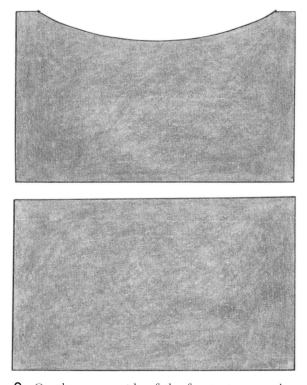

MAKING THE BUSINESS CARD HOLDER

1. Using the Business Card Holder pattern (see page 28) and a pen, trace 1 front and 1 back onto the wrong side of the leather. Use a snap blade cutter, cutting mat, and straight edge to cut out the two pieces.

2. On the wrong side of the front piece, apply a ¼" strip of adhesive transfer tape along the sides and bottom. Burnish the tape and peel off the paper backing.

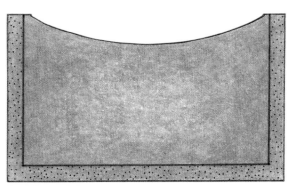

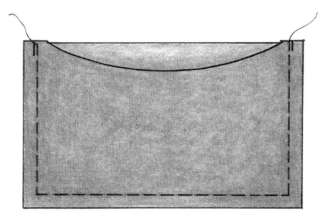

3. Placing wrong sides together, adhere the front piece to the back piece. Use your sewing machine to topstitch along the sides and bottom, ⅛" from the edge, back-tacking where you start and finish stitching.

4. Finish the edges of the leather by rubbing them with gum tragacanth or by applying acrylic paint.

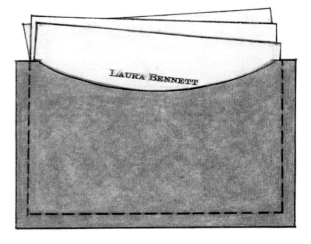

Business Card Holder Pattern
(Front / Back)
(shown at 100%)

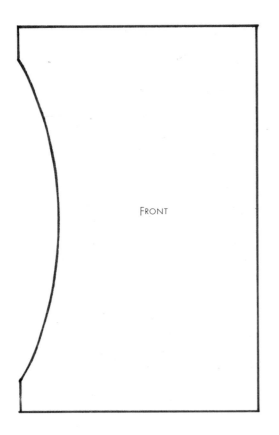

Front

Back

KEY RING TAB

Keep your keys together in style with this classic Key Ring Tab. Pair it with the Business Card Holder (page 26) and you have the perfect gift set for a business associate or for a recent graduate just entering the workforce.

MATERIALS

6" × 2½" piece 3-ounce leather
3M 465 adhesive transfer tape
Gum tragacanth or acrylic paint
Heavy-duty or all-purpose thread
Metal split key ring

TOOLS

Sewing machine
Size 14 or 16 leather sewing
   machine needles
Snap blade cutter
Self-healing cutting mat
Metal straight edge

MAKING THE KEY RING TAB

1. Use a ruler to find the midpoint of the 6" side of the piece of leather, and draw a line across the wrong side of the leather. Trace the Key Ring Tab pattern (next page) on one half of the wrong side of the leather.

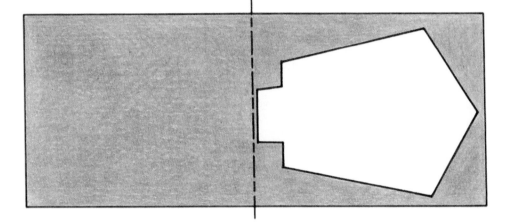

2. Apply adhesive transfer tape to cover the traced tab, leaving the upper loop. Burnish the tape and peel off the paper backing.

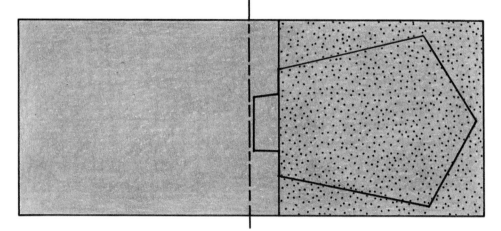

3. Fold the leather along the line drawn in step 1, and press to adhere the tape. Retrace the Key Ring Tab pattern on the right side of the leather, lining up the top edge of the tab pattern with the fold in the leather.

4. Starting in the middle of a long side, stitch ⅛" from the edge around all sides. End by overlapping three or four stitches.

5. Use a snap blade cutter, cutting mat, and straight edge to cut out the tab. Finish the edges of the leather by rubbing them with gum tragacanth or by applying acrylic paint. Insert the metal split key ring.

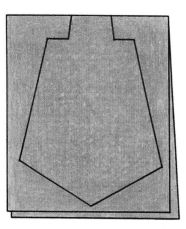

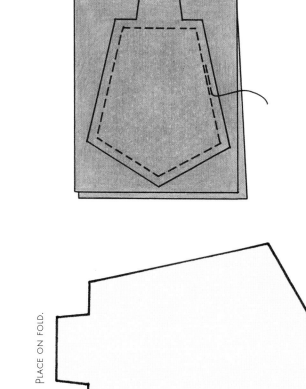

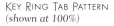

KEY RING TAB PATTERN
(shown at 100%)

PLACE ON FOLD.

KEY RING TASSEL

If you are looking for something more feminine and designer chic than the basic Key Ring Tab (page 29), try this super simple tassel. I recommend using a soft, thin leather, such as lambskin or calfskin, to prevent the stem from getting too bulky.

MATERIALS

13" x 3" strip of Ultrasuede

3M 465 adhesive transfer tape

Heavy-duty or all-purpose thread

Metal split key ring

Gum tragacanth or acrylic paint

TOOLS

Sewing machine

Size 14 or 16 leather sewing
    machine needles

Snap blade cutter

Self-healing cutting mat

Metal straight edge

Sharp scissors

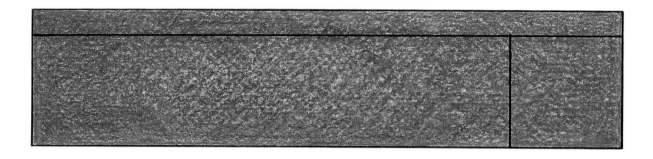

MAKING THE KEY RING TASSEL

1. Using a snap blade cutter, cutting mat, and straight edge, cut a rectangle of leather 3" × 13". On the wrong side of the leather, draw a line ½" from one long edge. (This will be the top edge of the tassel.) Then draw a vertical line 2½" from the right edge.

2. Cut away the smaller rectangle formed by these lines.

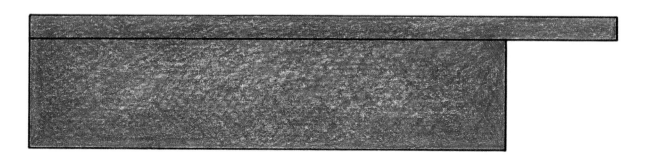

3. On the wrong side of the Ultrasuede, draw guidelines every inch or so.

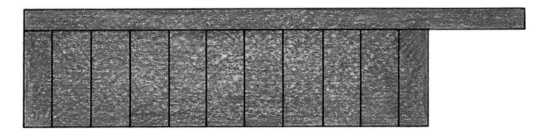

4. With a pair of sharp scissors, cut the folded Ultrasuede into thin strips approximately ⅛" wide. Stop at the ½" mark. (I usually cut the ⅛" strips by sight to avoid excessive pen markings on the leather.)

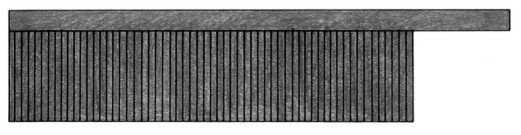

5. Cut a strip of Ultrasuede 1" × 4¾". Apply adhesive transfer tape to the entire wrong side. Burnish the tape and peel off the paper backing, and fold the piece in half lengthwise. Stitch ⅛" from the folded edge. Trim close to the stitching.

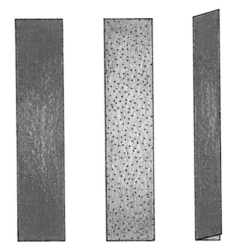

6. Fold the stitched strip in half and sew it to the upper left edge of the tassel body. This will form a loop after the tassel is completed. Apply a ½" strip of adhesive transfer tape along the entire length of the ½" section. Burnish the tape and peel off the paper backing.

7. Starting at the loop end, carefully roll up the tassel, keeping the top edge neat as you roll.

8. Insert the metal split key ring through the loop.

EYEGLASSES CASE WITH VARIATIONS

This pretty case is roomy enough for your eyeglasses and your sunglasses to cohabitate, or it will fit one pair of the biggest, most glamorous movie star glasses you can find. The basic project is simple, yet totally versatile. Just change the dimensions to make it larger or smaller, and try different hardware for endless variations: makeup bag, cell phone holder, or clutch. Using this simple construction technique, you are sure to come up with a handmade gift for everyone on your list.

MATERIALS

1 square foot
   3-ounce leather
3M 465 adhesive
   transfer tape
Twist turn-lock hardware
Heavy-duty or
   all-purpose thread
Gum tragacanth
   or acrylic paint

TOOLS

Sewing machine
Size 14 or 16 leather sewing
   machine needles
Snap blade cutter
Self-healing cutting mat
Metal straight edge
Screwdriver

MAKING THE EYEGLASSES CASE

1. Use a snap blade cutter, cutting mat, and straight edge to cut one 8" × 10¾" piece of leather for the body and one 8" × 3½" piece of leather for the cover lining.

2. Apply adhesive transfer tape to the entire wrong side of the cover-lining piece (the smaller rectangle). Burnish the tape and peel off the paper backing. Adhere the cover lining to the body piece along one 8" edge, aligning carefully.

3. Apply a ¼" strip of adhesive transfer tape to the body sides. Fold the body bottom edge up to just cover the lining edge.

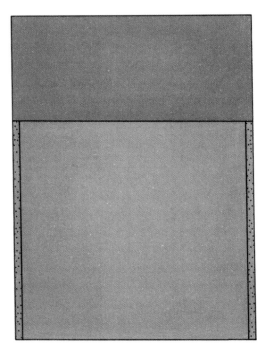

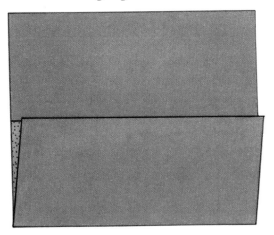

4. Beginning at the folded edge, stitch side seams ⅛" from the raw edges. Back-tack where you finish stitching. Turn the case over and topstitch the cover flap ⅛" from the edge. Be careful to align your starting and ending stitches with the side stitches.

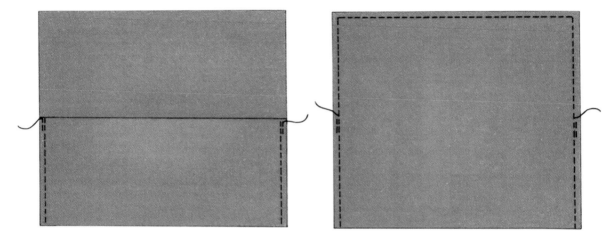

5. Working on the wrong side of the leather, mark the center of the flap. Place the bottom turn-lock plate there, positioning it ⅜" from the edge. Trace the opening in the plate. Remove the plate, use a snap blade cutter to cut out the opening, and install the turn-lock hardware using a small screwdriver to connect the bottom plate to the top plate.

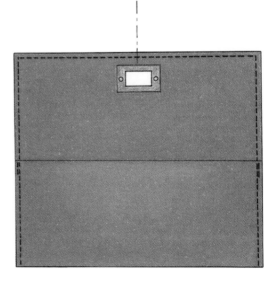

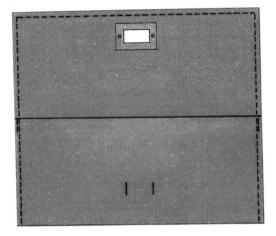

6. Fold the cover flap down and mark the placement of the turn portion of the lock. Use a snap blade cutter to cut slots for the hardware. Insert a piece of cardboard or the corner of a self-healing cutting mat to avoid going through to the bottom layer of leather. Insert the twist turn-lock, place the backplate on the wrong side of the leather, and fold the prongs outward. Finish the exposed edges with gum tragacanth or acrylic paint.

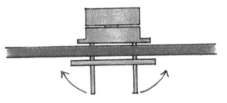

7. Cut a piece of leather large enough to cover the backplate and prongs on the inside of your case. Cover the wrong side of the leather with adhesive transfer tape. Burnish the tape and peel off the paper backing. Adhere the leather over the hardware inside the case to prevent your glasses from being scratched.

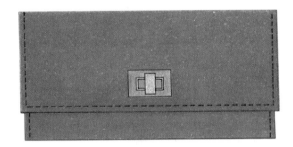

8. Now change the proportions or the hardware, and make a variation of your own!

Variations:

MAKE A CLUTCH

Use a 9" × 16" piece of leather for the body and a 9" × 5" piece of leather for the lining. If you would like to add a chain, stitch a 15" length of chain to each side at the fold. To add some color to the center of the clutch, stitch a 1" wide strip of leather in a contrasting color to the center of the body piece before you sew the side seams.

MAKE A CELL PHONE CASE

Use a 3¼" × 13" piece of leather for the body and a 3¼" × 3" piece of leather for the lining.

MAKE A MAKEUP BRUSH CASE

Use a 2¾" × 18" piece of leather for the body and a 2¾" × 3¾" piece of leather for the lining.

ZIPPER POUCH

This is another basic project with the potential for multiple variations. Use a zipper in a bold, contrasting color to make a statement, or keep it elegant by matching it to the leather or fabric you use for the body. Any size zipper will do; the length of the zipper you choose will determine the width of your pouch, so you can purchase a zipper of a particular size or use one you already have. Make a zipper pouch sized to fit inside the Eyeglasses Case, and you have just created a fabulous wallet. Add a smaller version of the Key Ring Tassel (page 32) to the zipper pull for a custom detail. Make a large pouch to use as a cosmetic bag or a small one to carry loose change. The possibilities are endless.

MATERIALS

3-ounce leather or heavy fabric

Zipper in the size and color desired

3M 465 adhesive transfer tape

Heavy-duty or all-purpose thread

Gum tragacanth or acrylic paint

TOOLS

Sewing machine

Size 14 or 16 leather sewing machine needles

Snap blade cutter

Self-healing cutting mat

Metal straight edge

MAKING THE ZIPPER POUCH

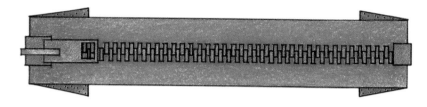

1. Fold under the ends of the zipper and adhere them to the wrong size of the zipper fabric with enough adhesive transfer tape to secure them.

2. Apply a strip of adhesive tape along the length of both sides of the top of the zipper.

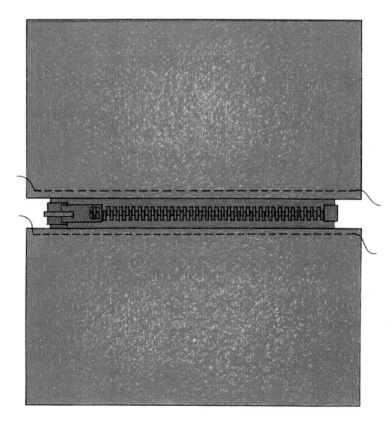

3. For the body of your pouch, use a snap blade cutter, cutting mat, and straight edge to cut two pieces of leather (or bias-cut heavy fabric) 1" longer than the zipper by whatever depth you want the pouch to be. Burnish the tape on the zipper and peel off the paper backing. Adhere the body pieces to the zipper right sides up and centered so that the body piece is ½" longer than the zipper on each end. Stitch ⅛" from the edge on both sides of the zipper. Back-tack where you start and finish stitching.

4. Working on the wrong side of the leather, apply strips of adhesive transfer tape to the sides and bottom of one of the body pieces. Burnish the tape and peel off the paper backing.

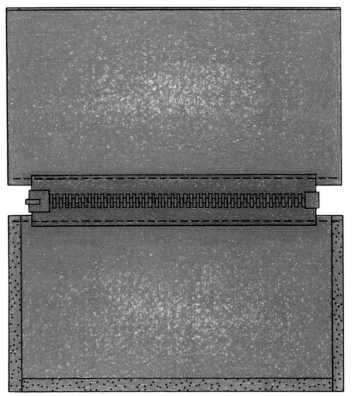

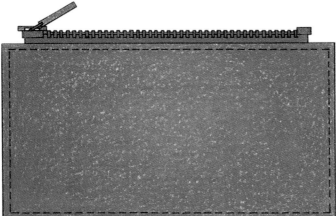

5. Carefully line up and adhere the edges of the two body sides. Stitch 1/8" from the edge. If you have used leather, finish the edges with gum tragacanth or acrylic paint. Bias cut fabric will fray slightly with use.

Classic Chain Belt

This wardrobe essential adds a classic touch to any outfit. It's adjustable, so it's easy to wear with jeans, skirts, or even with a suit when you want to pretend to be a lady who lunches.

The materials for this project can be purchased at any bead or craft store or can easily be found online. Any style or weight of chain will work; just make sure that your clasp is proportionate to the chain you choose. Lobster clasps come in many styles, from plain to fancy, and the ½-inch size used here is just a suggestion. If the chain you choose is chunky, you may need a larger clasp; just make sure the clasp you select can close around one of the links. Similarly, the jump rings (small rings used to connect lengths of chain or charms) should be large enough to connect two links or to connect your charm to a link of your chain. Most needle-nose pliers have wire-cutting edges near the back of their tapered jaws, but if yours do not, you will need a separate pair of wire cutters.

MATERIALS

57" chain
½" lobster claw clasp
6 jump rings, ¼" each
Charm

TOOLS

Needle nose pliers
    with wire cutting edges
    (or separate wire cutters,
    if necessary)

MAKING THE CLASSIC CHAIN BELT

1. Using the pliers or wire cutters, cut three pieces of chain: a 36" piece, a 10" piece, and an 11" piece.

2. Open a jump ring by gently twisting it with the pliers. After passing the open ring through a link at one end of the 36" piece and then the lobster claw clasp, use the pliers to squeeze it closed.

3. Use jump rings to attach the 10" and 11" pieces of chain to the same link as the lobster claw clasp on the 36" piece of chain.

4. Use a ruler to measure 8½" from the end of the
36" chain. Attach the free ends of the 10" and 11"
pieces of chain to this same link.

5. Use a jump ring to attach the charm to the link
on the opposite end of the 36" piece.

WIDE CUFF BRACELET
WITH BELT VARIATION

Bold and striking, these wide bracelets and belts are statement pieces sure to draw attention. Whether you prefer to wear your belts high on your waist or lower on your hip, you can custom-fit this belt by measuring exactly where you want it to sit. Purchased bracelets are generally 7½ to 8 inches long, so you can start around there, but feel free to custom-fit these also, if your wrists are unusually large or small.

MATERIALS

FOR THE BRACELET: 1 square foot 3- to 4-ounce leather

FOR THE BELT: 3 square feet 3- to 4-ounce leather

2 sets push button lock hardware (one each for the bracelet and the belt)

3M 465 adhesive transfer tape

Gum tragacanth or acrylic paint

Heavy-duty or all-purpose thread

Masking tape

TOOLS

Sewing machine

Size 14 or 16 leather sewing machine needles

Snap blade cutter

Self-healing cutting mat

Metal straight edge

Needle-nose pliers

Flexible tape measure

MAKING THE WIDE CUFF BRACELET

1. Using a snap blade cutter, cutting mat, and straight edge, cut two strips of leather, each 1⅞" × 8". Apply adhesive transfer tape to the entire wrong side of one strip.

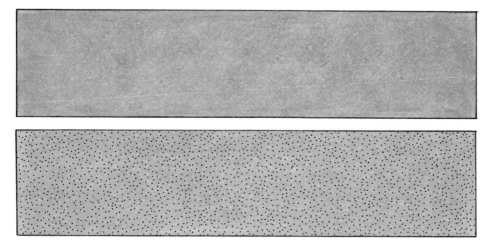

2. Burnish the tape and peel off the paper backing. Placing wrong sides together, press to adhere the two strips. Topstitch ⅛" from one long edge, stopping ¾" from one end. Back-tack and repeat on the other long edge.

3. Cover the hasp of the hardware with several layers of masking tape to avoid scratching it while you install it. Position the hasp on one short end of the leather strip and use the pliers to apply gradual, even pressure along the length of the hasp.

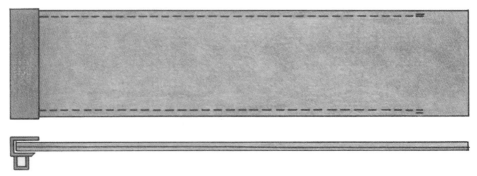

4. Using the bottom plate provided with the hardware, mark the placement for the prong slots for the clasp. Peel back the bottom layer of leather and cut slots in the top layer only.

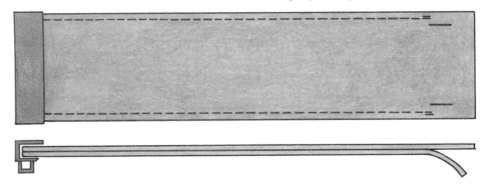

5. Push the prongs of the hardware through the slots and bend them inward. (Do not use the bottom plate provided.) Re-adhere the bottom and top layers of leather. Finish the edges of the leather with gum tragacanth or acrylic paint.

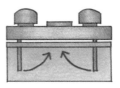

Variation:

MAKE IT A BELT

Place the flexible tape measure around your waist where you would like the belt to sit. Add ¼" to that measurement to account for the hardware overlap. Cut two pieces of leather, each 1⅞" wide and as long as the measurement you calculated. Follow steps 2 through 5 on pages 49 to 50 to complete the belt.

Drop Lock Bracelet
with Belt Variation

The medium width of this bracelet and belt makes them the most versatile of all: perfect for all body types and personal styles.

MATERIALS

FOR THE BRACELET: 1 square foot 3- to 4-ounce leather

FOR THE BELT: 3 square feet 3- to 4-ounce leather

Drop lock hardware

3M 465 adhesive transfer tape

Gum tragacanth or acrylic paint

Heavy-duty or all-purpose thread

TOOLS

Sewing machine

Size 14 or 16 leather sewing machine needles

Snap blade cutter

Self-healing cutting mat

Metal straight edge

Leather hole punch

Small screwdriver

Flexible tape measure

MAKING THE DROP LOCK BRACELET

1. Using a snap blade cutter, cutting mat, and straight edge, cut two strips of leather, each 1" × 8½". Apply adhesive transfer tape to the entire wrong side of one strip.

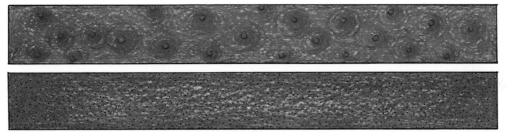

2. Burnish the tape and peel off the paper backing. Placing wrong sides together, press to adhere the two strips. Topstitch ⅛" from the edge around all four sides.

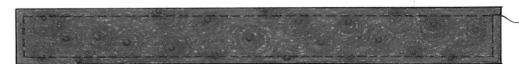

3. Place the slotted bottom plate on the underside of the leather strip (what will be the wrong side of the bracelet). Line it up with the short edge. The width of the plate should be the same as the width of the strip. Trace the openings and the locations of the screw holes. Cut out the slots with a snap blade cutter. Use a leather hole punch to punch holes for the screws. Use a small screwdriver to install the hardware.

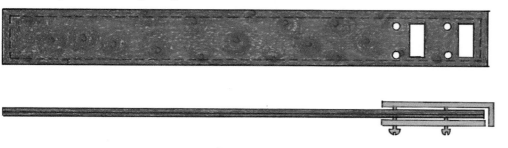

4. Place the folding lock portion of the hardware ¼" from the opposite end of the bracelet and mark the position of the prong slots. Cut out the slots with a snap blade cutter.

5. Insert the prongs of the hardware into the slots and bend them inward. Do not install the bottom plate provided with the folding lock. Finish the edges of the leather with gum tragacanth or acrylic paint.

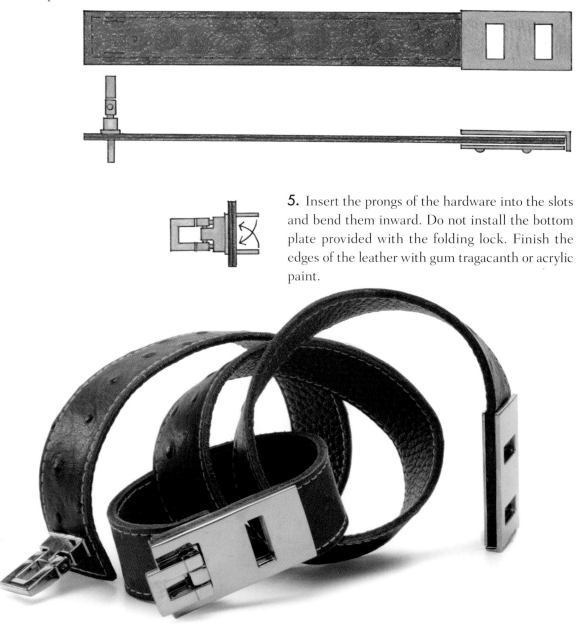

Variation:

MAKE IT A BELT

Use a flexible tape measure to measure around your waist where you would like the belt to sit, and add ½" to account for the hardware overlap. From a 3 square feet 3- to 4-ounce piece of leather, cut two strips of leather, each 1" wide and as long as the measurement you calculated. Follow steps 2 through 5 on pages 52 to 53 to complete the Drop Lock Belt.

WRAP BRACELET
WITH BELT VARIATION

When the tiniest detail will do, add a narrow bracelet or belt. These Wrap pieces have a distinct equestrian style.

MATERIALS

FOR THE BRACELET: 2 ½" x 19" strips of 3-ounce leather
Two ½" snap hooks
FOR THE BELT: 2 ½" x 65" strips of 3-ounce leather
Two ½" snap hooks
One 1" strap loop

3M 465 transfer adhesive tape

Heavy-duty or all-purpose thread

Gum tragacanth or acrylic paint

TOOLS

Sewing machine

Size 14 or 16 leather sewing machine needles

Snap blade cutter

Self-healing cutting mat

Metal straight edge

Small screwdriver

Flexible tape measure

MAKING THE WRAP BRACELET

1. Using a snap blade cutter, cutting mat, and straight edge, cut two strips of leather, one ½" × 19" and one ½" × 17". Apply adhesive transfer tape to the entire wrong side of the shorter strip.

2. Burnish the tape and peel off the paper backing. Adhere the strips to one another, wrong sides together. Topstitch along the length of each side, ⅛" from the edge.

3. Fold the ends of the stitched strap through the loops of the snap hooks. Sew across and back-tack all stitches.

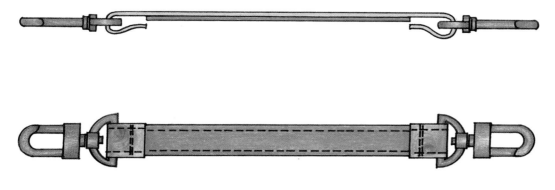

Variation:

MAKE IT A BELT

Use a flexible tape measure to measure around your waist where you would like the belt to sit. Double that measurement, and add 2 inches. Cut one strip of leather ½" wide and as long as the measurement you calculated and one 2" shorter. Follow steps 2 and 3 of the wrap bracelet on page 57. Place a 1" strap loop in the center of the belt. Fold the prongs outward and do not use the backplate provided.

Note: To make a strip of leather long enough for the wrap belt, you can piece together strips. Just be sure to stagger the places where two pieces of leather meet (the joints) so that a joint on one layer is on top of a solid section of the bottom layer, and vice versa. The center of the top piece is a good spot to place a joint because it will be hidden by the hardware.

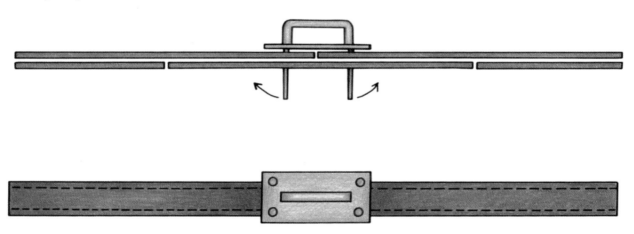

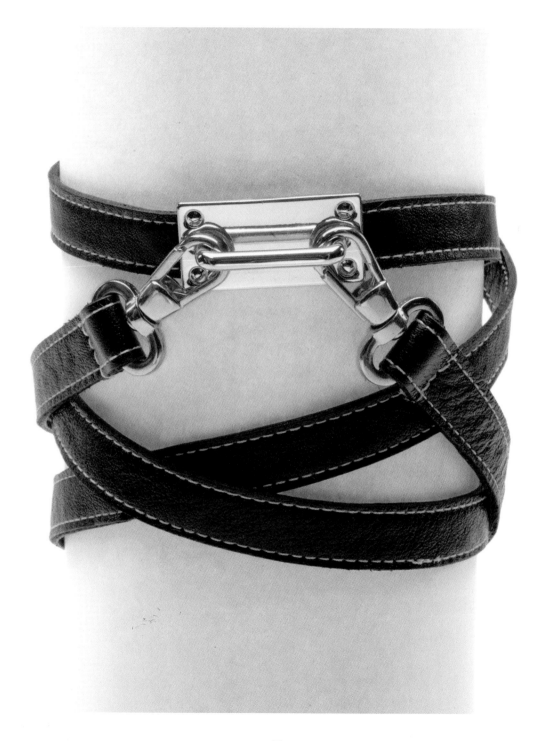

section II FASHIONABLY

ORGA

NIZED

Traditionally, we've thought of fashion accessories as hand-

bags, shoes, and belts. But as we grow more dependent on

(read: addicted to) our personal electronics, the materials we

choose to protect and cover them with become an extension

of our personalities and our outfits. In short, our electronics

have become our new fashion accessories. A friend of mine

received an e-tablet for Mother's Day and admitted she was

more excited to shop for a cover than to actually use the

e-tablet. If you aren't big on electronics, fear not: This section

also contains projects for those of us who still read books

and write on paper.

INSPIRATION . . .

. . . TO ORGANIZE

BOOK COVER

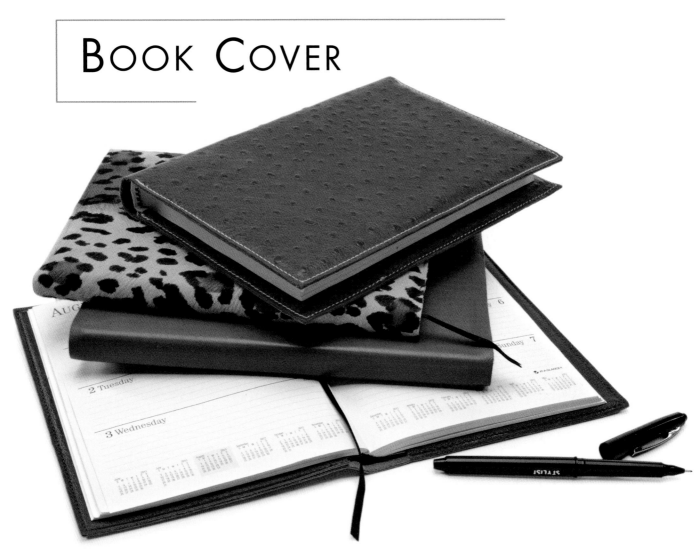

Preserve a favorite novel or a cherished book from your childhood with a beautiful cover made of leather or heavy-weight fabric. This project is also a great way to make a plain photo album or scrapbook as special as the memories captured within it.

MATERIALS

2 square feet 3-ounce leather

3M 465 adhesive transfer tape

Heavy-duty or all-purpose thread

Gum tragacanth or acrylic paint

TOOLS

Sewing machine

Size 14 or 16 leather sewing machine needles

Snap blade cutter

Self-healing cutting mat

Metal straight edge

Tape measure

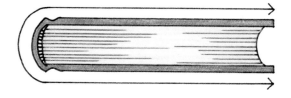

MAKING THE BOOK COVER

1. Using a tape measure, measure across the front cover, around the spine, and across the back cover of the book for which you are making the cover. Add 1" to this total measurement. This is the width of your book cover.

2. Measure from the top edge of the book to the bottom edge. Add ½" to this measurement. This is the height of your book cover.

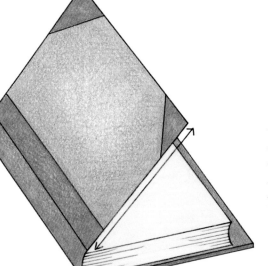

3. Open the book and measure the inside front cover from the outside edge to the gutter. Add ¼" to this measurement. This total measurement by the book height (see step 2) will be the front and back flap dimensions for your book cover.

4. Using a snap blade cutter, cutting mat, and straight edge, cut one piece of leather or fabric with the height and width dimensions you calculated in steps 1 and 2. Cut two pieces of leather or fabric with the dimensions you calculated in step 3.

5. On the wrong side of one book flap piece, apply a ¼" strip of adhesive transfer tape to the top, bottom, and outside edges. Repeat with the other book flap piece.

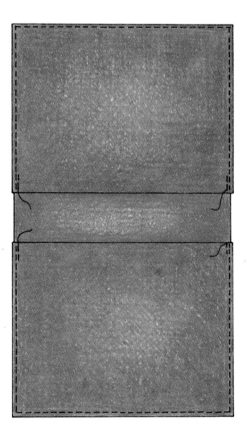

6. Burnish the tape and peel off the paper backing. Adhere the flaps to the book cover body. Topstitch ⅛" from the outer edges of the book flaps, back-tacking where you start and finish stitching. Finish the edges with gum tragacanth or acrylic paint.

PUSH LOCK LAPTOP ENVELOPE

Protect your laptop in style with this high-end leather envelope. Made by simply folding a length of leather and sewing just two seams, this simple piece is ready for the designer-look hardware of your choice. A computer that keeps you organized and connected to the world doesn't deserve anything less than this chic envelope.

MATERIALS

Piece of 3-ounce leather approximately 12" × 34"

3M 465 adhesive transfer tape

Push lock hardware

Heavy-duty or all-purpose thread

Gum tragacanth or acrylic paint

TOOLS

Sewing machine

Size 14 or 16 leather sewing machine needles

Snap blade cutter

Self-healing cutting mat

Metal straight edge

Flexible tape measure

Small screwdriver

MAKING THE PUSH LOCK LAPTOP ENVELOPE

1. Use a tape measure to measure all the way around your computer. Add 2" to this total measurement, then divide by 2. This is the width of your envelope piece.

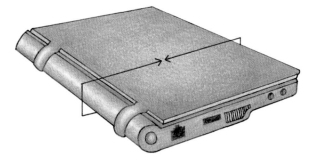

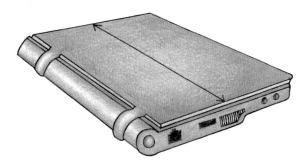

2. Measure the front, one short side, and the back of your computer. Add 5" to this total measurement. This is the length of your envelope piece.

3. Using a snap blade cutter, cutting mat, and straight edge, cut a piece of leather with the dimensions you calculated in steps 1 and 2. Cut a flap lining piece 5" long and the width of the envelope piece.

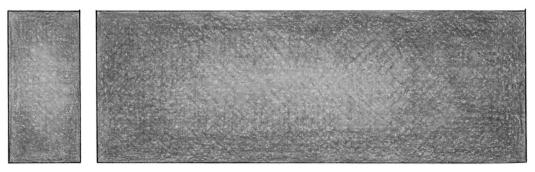

4. Apply adhesive transfer tape to the entire wrong side of the flap lining. Burnish the tape and peel off the paper backing, and adhere it to the body piece. Apply ¼" strips of adhesive transfer tape along the edges of the body piece.

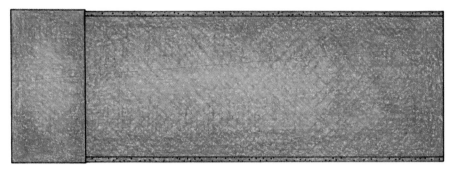

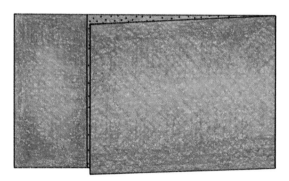

5. Fold the body piece over to meet the cover flap and carefully line up the edges.

6. Topstitch along the sides of the body piece ⅛" from the edge, stopping where the envelope meets the flap. Back-tack where you start and finish stitching.

7. Turn the piece over and topstitch around the flap ⅛" from edge.

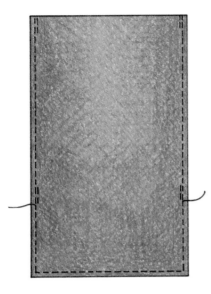

8. Install the hasp portion of the push lock hardware on the flap by placing it in the center and securing it, using a small screwdriver and the screws provided.

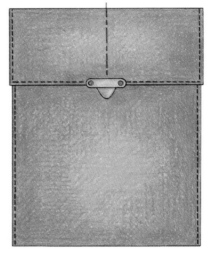

9. Install the push lock portion of the hardware by marking the slot positions using the backplate. (Do this by attaching the two pieces of the hardware together and marking where the push lock portion falls on the leather.) Cut out the slots, insert the tabs, and put the backplate in position. Bend the tabs outward. Cut a piece of leather slightly larger than the backplate. Cover the wrong side of the piece with adhesive transfer tape. Burnish the tape and peel off the paper backing, and adhere it to the back of the hardware to prevent it from scratching your computer. Finish the edges with gum tragacanth or acrylic paint.

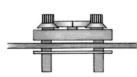

BELTED LAPTOP ENVELOPE

Just slightly more complex than the simple laptop envelope, this project involves a change of hardware and the addition of a strap that functions as the closure.

MATERIALS

4 square feet 3-ounce leather (you will need to cut a piece approximately 12" × 34")

3M 465 transfer adhesive tape

1" strap loop

Two 1" snap hooks

Heavy-duty or all-purpose thread

Gum tragacanth or acrylic paint

TOOLS

Sewing machine

Size 14 or 16 leather sewing machine needles

Snap blade cutter

Self-healing cutting mat

Metal straight edge

Small screwdriver

Flexible tape measure

MAKING THE BELTED LAPTOP ENVELOPE

1. Follow steps 1 to 3 for the Push Lock Laptop Envelope (see page 68). Draw a line on the wrong side of the leather, 5" from one short edge. Beginning at this line, apply ¼" strips of adhesive tape to the long edges of the piece. Fold the body piece up to this line and carefully line up the edges.

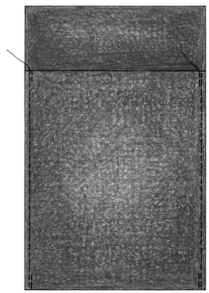

2. Topstitch along the sides of the body piece, ⅛" from the edge, stopping where the envelope meets the flap. Back-tack where you start and finish stitching.

3. Turn the piece over, and measure and mark the center point on the laptop envelope flap. Place the 1" strap loop in the center of the flap and ¾" from the edge. Mark the slot placement for the prongs. Cut the slots using a snap blade cutter and cutting mat. Insert the prongs through the slots and position the backplate. Fold the prongs outward.

4. Apply adhesive transfer tape to completely cover the back of the flap lining piece. Burnish the tape and peel off the paper backing, and adhere it to the wrong side of the flap piece. Topstitch around the flap ⅛" from the edge.

5. With the flap folded down, measure around the envelope starting at one side of the strap loop hardware, around the back, and to the other end of the strap loop.

6. Using the measurement in step 5, cut one ½" strip of leather and one ½" strip 2" shorter. Completely cover the wrong side of short strip with adhesive transfer tape. Burnish the tape and peel off the paper backing, and adhere the two strips together. Topstitch ⅛" from the edge along both lengths. Fold the ends of the stitched strap through the loops of the snap hooks. Sew across and backtack all stitches.

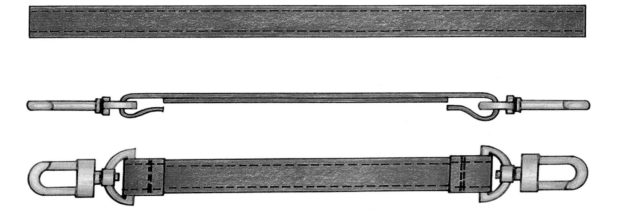

7. Slip your computer into the envelope, and then place this strap over the circle hardware and around the computer case. Turn the case over and mark spots above and below the strap, ½" from the edges of the case. Remove the strap and insert the corner of a self-healing mat into the envelope. Use a snap blade cutter to cut from the upper to the lower dot on each side.

8. From the inside of the case, push the strap ends through these cuts and wrap the strap around the front of the computer to meet the strap loop. Finish the edges with gum tragacanth or acrylic paint.

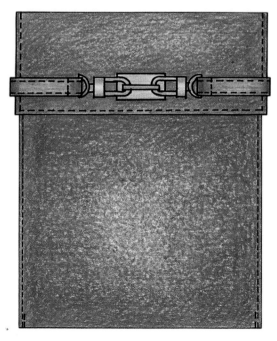

QUILTED LAPTOP CASE

My laptop is my lifeline, so I tend to be very careful about how it gets transported. This case protects as well as a store-bought case, but with loads more style. The batting and secure closure will keep your baby safe and warm. Quilted cases to protect your laptop are available just about anywhere, but you can create this beyond-fabulous one by using an unusual fabric combination.

MATERIALS

1 yard fabric for the cover

1 yard light to medium weight contrasting fabric for the lining and binding

1 yard quilt batting

Snap or Velco closure

All-purpose thread

TOOLS

Sewing machine

Hand sewing needles

Flexible measuring tape

Fabric scissors

Pins

Tailor's chalk or fabric marker

MAKING THE QUILTED LAPTOP CASE

1. Use a yardstick or tape measure to measure across the front of your computer. Add 5" to this measurement. This is your cut fabric width.

2. Measure from the front edge to the back, around the hinge, and back to the front edge of your computer. Add 10" to this total measurement. This is your fabric length.

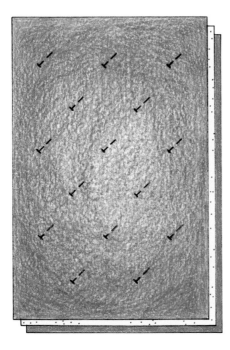

3. Cut one piece each of your cover fabric, lining fabric, and quilt batting with the dimensions you calculated in steps 1 and 2. Layer the pieces together by putting the lining fabric right side down, the batting on top of the lining, and then the cover fabric on top, right side up. Use pins to hold the layers in place, spacing them across the entire surface of your quilt layers.

4. Fold down one corner of the three layers and align the top edges of the corner and the quilt lay-ers. Insert a yardstick into the crease. Open the fold and trace the edge of the yardstick with chalk or a fabric marker.

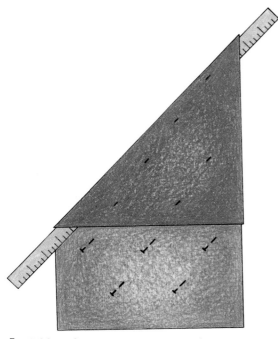

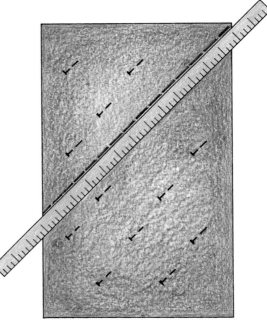

5. Fold in the opposite corner and repeat step 4.

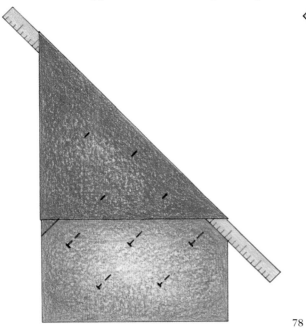

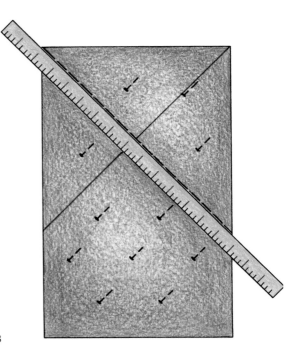

6. Stitch the lines that form the X. Remove the piece from your machine and use chalk or a fabric marker to mark lines 1" apart. Stitch on the marked lines, changing direction with each line of stitching and working from the center out until the entire piece is covered.

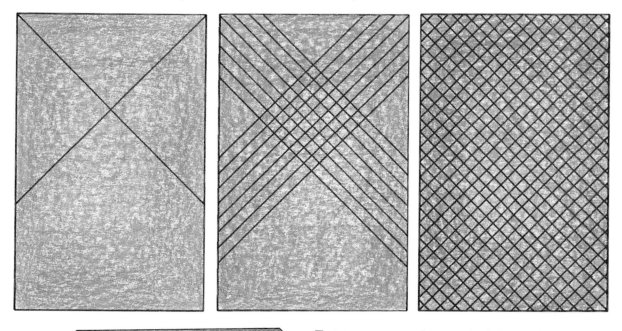

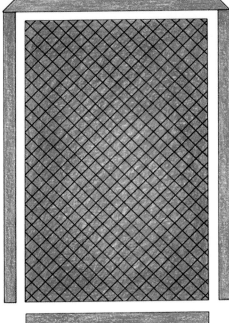

7. Measure one short end of the quilted piece. From the lining fabric, bias cut a strip that length and 1" wide. Measure around the remaining sides (two long and one short) of your piece and add 2" to this measurement. From the lining fabric, bias cut a strip that length and 1" wide. This will be used in step 11.

8. Pin the short bias strip right-side down across the quilted fabric edge. Sew using a ¼" seam allowance. Fold the strip up, then turn down the top edge to meet the top of the fabric quilt.

9. Turn the piece over, fold the strip around the raw edges of the fabric layers, and whipstitch the edge of the strip to the quilted lining.

10. Place your computer on the lining side of the quilted fabric and fold the bottom up to meet the top edge of your computer. Pin the sides of the fabric to fit the computer snugly and use your machine to sew the seams. Trim the seam allowances to ¼". Fold down the flap and trim it to your desired length. Round off the top corners.

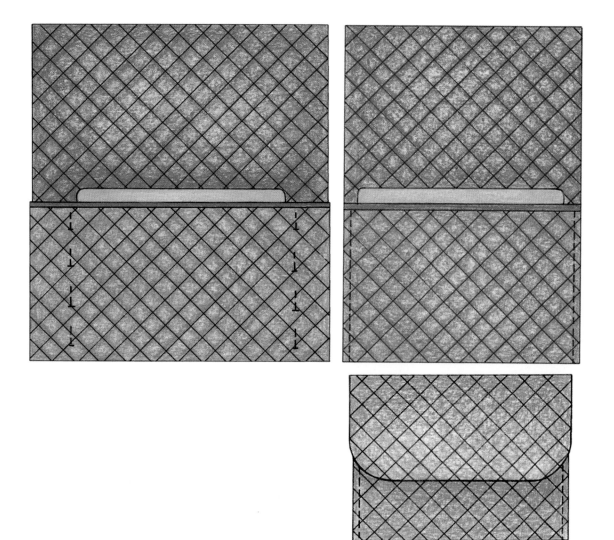

11. Fold in the ends of the long bias strip by 1". Pin the strip right side down along the sides and top of the quilted fabric, aligning the raw edges. Use your sewing machine to attach the binding using a ¼" seam allowance.

12. Turn the piece over, fold the strip over the raw edges of the quilted fabric, and whipstitch the edge of the strip in place.

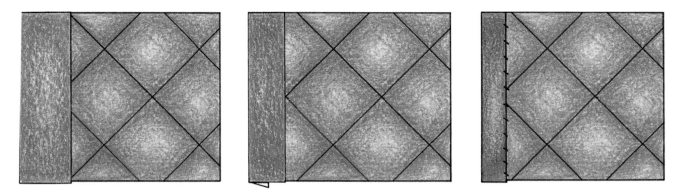

13. Use the yardstick or tape measure to find the center of the flap edge, and measure 1" in from the edge. Stitch on a snap or Velcro closure in this spot and in the coordinating spot on the body of the computer case.

CHECKBOOK COVER

My husband doesn't want an E-ZPass to automatically pay road tolls because he says that's how Big Brother can monitor his comings and goings. While my life is not nearly exciting enough for anyone to monitor, I am wary of automatic deductions from my bank account, so I still use checks to pay my bills. And why wouldn't I? In this gorgeous checkbook cover, my checks look fabulous.

MATERIALS

1 square foot 3-ounce leather for the cover

1 square foot 1-ounce contrasting-color leather for the lining

Plastic or vinyl folder

3M 465 adhesive transfer tape

Heavy-duty or all-purpose thread

Gum tragacanth or acrylic paint

TOOLS

Sewing machine

Size 14 or 16 leather sewing machine needles

Sewing machine zipper foot

Snap blade cutter

Self-healing cutting mat

Metal straight edge

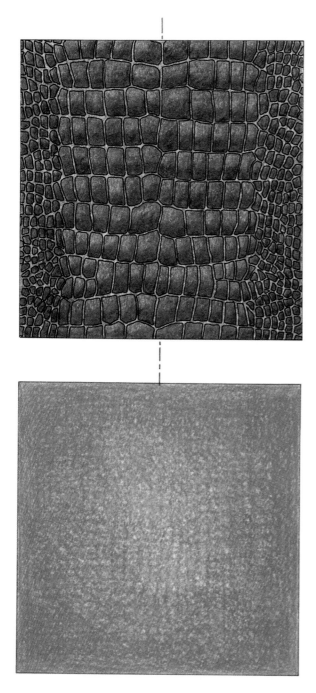

MAKING THE CHECKBOOK COVER

1. Use a snap blade cutter, cutting mat, and straight edge to cut one 6¾" × 7¼" piece from the cover leather and one 6¾" × 7¼" piece from the lining leather. If you're using patterned leather for the cover, be sure to center the design when you measure and mark.

2. Cut two 3" × 6" pieces out of the folder. Apply adhesive transfer tape to completely cover the backs of both pieces of plastic. Burnish the tape and peel off the paper backing, and adhere the plastic pieces to the wrong side of the cover leather, ½" from the bottom, top, and sides. The space in the middle will be larger than ½".

3. Place the Checkbook Template (see opposite page) on the wrong side of the cover leather and trace the rectangle. Remove the template and apply adhesive transfer tape to the entire wrong side of the cover leather, except inside this rectangle.

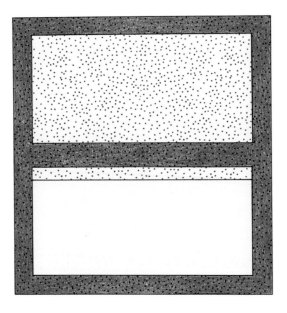

4. Place the Checkbook Template on the wrong side of the lining leather and cut along the top edge of the rectangle with a snap blade cutter. This will form the slit that the checkbook slips into.

5. Burnish the tape and peel off the paper backing. Adhere the wrong side of the lining leather to the wrong side of the cover leather. Topstitch close to the edge of the plastic. I find it helps to replace your regular sewing machine foot with a zipper foot and use the edge of the foot as a guide for this step. Alternatively, you could move your machine's needle to the far right (if your machine has this option) and use the edge of your regular presser foot as a guide.

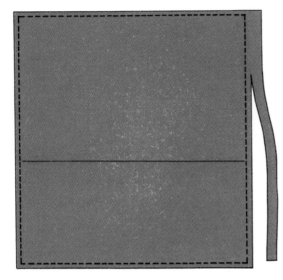

6. Use a snap blade cutter, cutting mat, and straight edge to trim the leather ⅛" from the stitching on all sides.

7. Fold the checkbook cover and burnish the crease. Finish the edges with gum tragacanth or acrylic paint. Insert a standard-size checkbook into the slot.

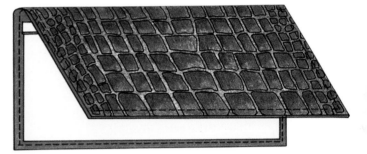

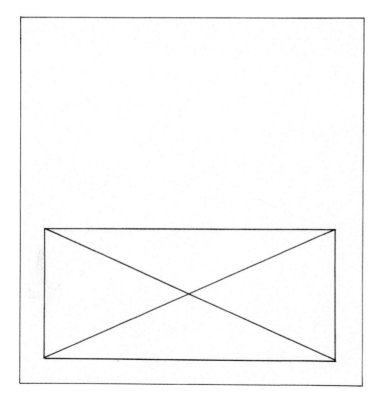

CHECKBOOK PATTERN
(shown at 50%)

FLIP NOTEBOOK

This luxurious little cover, made to accommodate a simple 3" x 5" spiral notebook, is small enough to keep in your pocket or purse, so keep one right at hand to jot down fleeting thoughts. I can't think of a more fashionable place to write down everything from golf scores to grocery lists.

MATERIALS

½ square foot 3-ounce leather for the cover

½ square foot 1-ounce leather for the lining

Plastic or vinyl folder

3" × 5" spiral flip notebook

3M 465 adhesive transfer tape

Heavy-duty or all-purpose thread

Gum tragacanth or acrylic paint

TOOLS

Sewing machine

Size 14 or 16 leather sewing machine needles

Sewing machine zipper foot

Snap blade cutter

Self-healing cutting mat

Metal straight edge

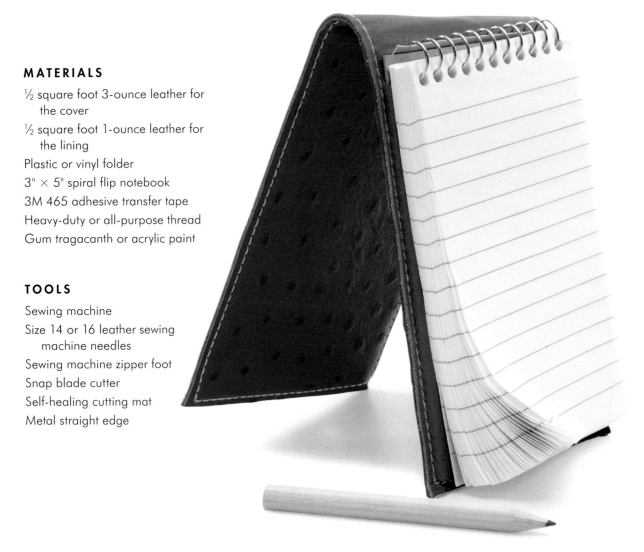

MAKING THE FLIP NOTEBOOK

1. Use a snap blade cutter, cutting mat, and straight edge to cut one 3½" × 11½" piece from the cover leather and one 3½" × 11½" piece from the lining leather.

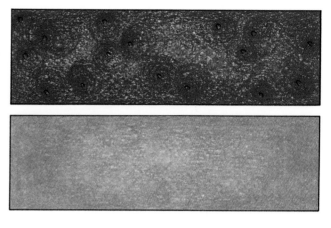

2. Cut two 3" × 5" pieces out of the folder. Apply adhesive transfer tape to completely cover the backs of both pieces of plastic. Burnish the tape and peel off the paper backing, and adhere the pieces of plastic to the wrong side of the cover leather ¼" from the bottom, top, and sides. The space in the middle will be larger than ¼".

3. Apply adhesive transfer tape to the entire wrong side of the cover, except for on the right-hand piece of plastic.

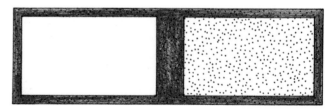

4. On the right side of the lining leather, make a cut 6⅝" from the right hand edge, stopping ¼" from the top and bottom edges. This is the slit that the notebook will slip into.

5. Burnish the tape and peel off the paper backing from the wrong side of the cover. Adhere the lining leather to the cover leather. Topstitch around all four sides of the cover close to the edge of the plastic (approximately ¼" from the edge of the leather). I find it helps to replace your regular sewing machine foot with a zipper foot and use the edge of the foot as a guide for this step. Alternatively, you could move your machine's needle to the far right (if your machine has this option) and use the edge of your regular presser foot as a guide.

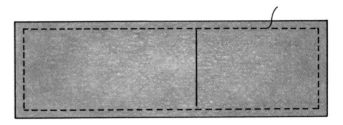

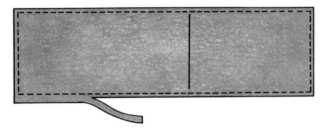

6. Use a snap blade cutter, cutting mat, and straight edge to trim the leather ⅛" from the stitching on all sides.

7. Fold the notebook cover in half and burnish the crease. Finish the edges with gum tragacanth or acrylic paint. Slip the 3" × 5" spiral flip notebook into the slot.

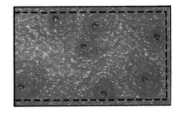

REFILLABLE NOTEPAD

This clever notepad cover elevates an everyday junior legal pad, available at any office supply store, to spectacular gift status. This project makes the perfect holiday present for a teacher, a co-worker, or anyone else on your list.

MATERIALS

1 square foot 3-ounce leather for the cover

1 square foot 1-ounce leather for the lining

Plastic or vinyl folder

5" × 8" junior legal pad

3M 465 adhesive transfer tape

Heavy-duty or all-purpose thread

Gum tragacanth or acrylic paint

TOOLS

Sewing machine

Size 14 or 16 leather sewing machine needles

Sewing machine zipper foot

Snap blade cutter

Self-healing cutting mat

Metal straight edge

MAKING THE REFILLABLE NOTEPAD

1. Use a snap blade cutter, cutting mat, and straight edge to cut one 9" × 11¾" piece from the cover leather and one 9" × 11¾" piece from the lining leather.

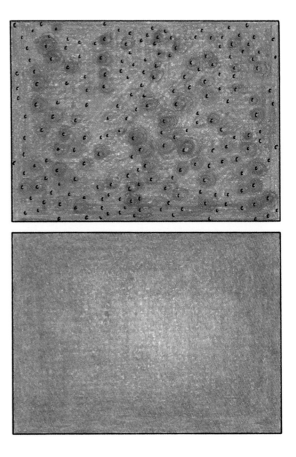

2. Cut two 5" × 8" pieces out of the folder. Apply adhesive transfer tape to completely cover the backs of both pieces of plastic. Burnish the tape and peel off the paper backing, and adhere the plastic pieces to the wrong side of the cover leather ½" from the bottom, top, and sides. The space in the middle will be larger than ½".

3. Apply adhesive transfer tape to the entire wrong side of the cover, except for the right-hand piece of plastic.

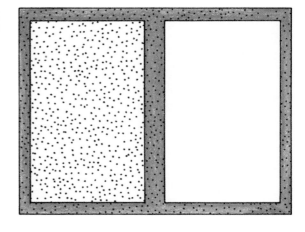

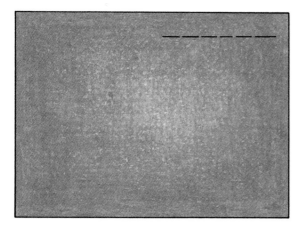

4. On the right side of the lining leather, make a 5" cut 1¼" from the top and ½" from the right edge. This is the slit that the notepad will slip into.

5. Burnish the tape and peel off the paper backing. Adhere the lining leather to the cover leather. Use a zipper foot to topstitch around all four sides of the cover close to the edge of the plastic (approximately ¼" from the edge of the leather).

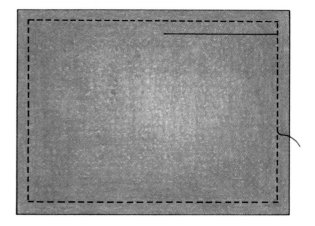

6. Use a snap blade cutter, cutting mat, and straight edge to trim the leather ⅛" from the stitching on all four sides.

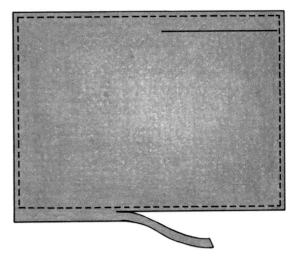

7. Fold the notebook cover in half and burnish the crease. Finish the edges with gum tragacanth or acrylic paint. Slip the 5" × 8" junior legal notepad into the slot.

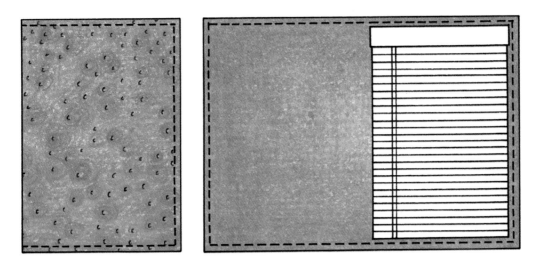

E-TABLET AND E-READER COVERS

E-TABLET COVER

MATERIALS

2 square feet 3-ounce leather for the cover

2 square feet 1-ounce leather for the lining

Plastic or vinyl folder

5" × 8" index card or piece of card stock

3M 465 adhesive transfer tape

Clear tablet gel skin

Heavy-duty or all-purpose thread

Gum tragacanth or acrylic paint

Masking tape

TOOLS

Sewing machine

Size 14 or 16 leather sewing machine needles

Snap blade cutter

Self-healing cutting mat

Metal straight edge

If you are in search of a phenomenal handmade man-gift, search no further. The beauty of these covers is that they not only look elegant, they are also fully functional. When you insert your device into them, you can access every button, slide, lock, and port. How do I achieve such a feat of engineering? By cheating, of course. These projects require a protective gel skin that slips onto the back of the device. These gel skins are sold at electronics stores or wherever you purchased your device. Choose the semi-rigid or soft gel covers, not the hard plastic kind, and get a clear or translucent color that you can see through in order to make some marks. If you are giving the cover as a gift, save the cardboard picture that comes in the gel skin to slip back into your final cover. It makes for a much nicer presentation.

MAKING THE E-TABLET COVER

1. Cut one 11" × 17" piece from the cover leather and one 11" × 17" piece from the lining leather.

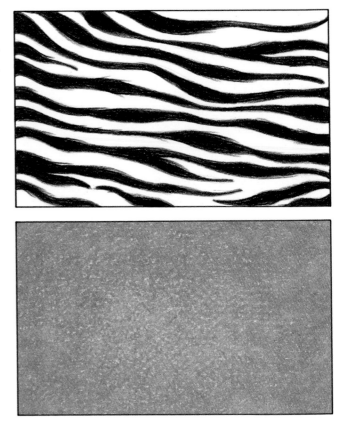

2. Cut two 7¼" × 10" pieces out of the folder. Apply adhesive transfer tape to completely cover the backs of both pieces of plastic. Burnish the tape and peel off the paper backing, and adhere the pieces of plastic to the wrong side of the cover leather ½" from the bottom, top, and sides. The space in the middle will be larger than ½".

3. On the wrong side of the lining leather, place the 5" × 8" card 1½" from the top edge and 1⅞" from the side edge. Trace the two long edges of the card.

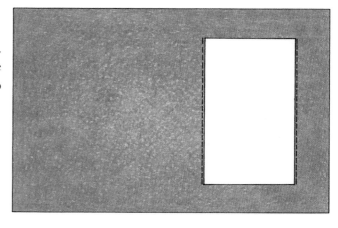

4. Draw a horizontal line to join the midpoints of the two lines, forming an H. Use a snap blade cutter to cut along these lines. This forms the tabs that will hold your gel cover in place.

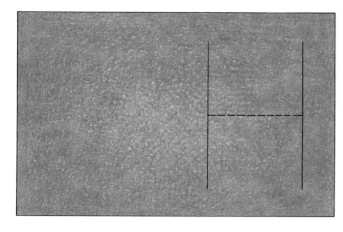

5. Place the 5" × 8" index card on the wrong side of the cover leather piece 1½" from the top edge and 1⅞" from the right edge. Trace around all four sides of the card. Apply adhesive transfer tape to the entire wrong side of the cover leather, except inside this rectangle.

6. Burnish the tape and peel off the paper backing. Adhere the wrong side of the lining leather to the wrong side of the cover leather. (It adds stability if you use masking tape to keep the letter H closed on the right side of the lining leather during this step.) Topstitch around all four sides close to the edge of the plastic (approximately ¼" from the edge). I find it helps to replace your regular sewing machine foot with a zipper foot and use the edge of the foot as a guide for this step. Alternatively, you could move your machine's needle to the far right (if your machine has this option) and use the edge of your regular presser foot as a guide. Use a snap blade cutter, cutting mat, and straight edge to trim the leather ⅛" from the stitching on all four sides.

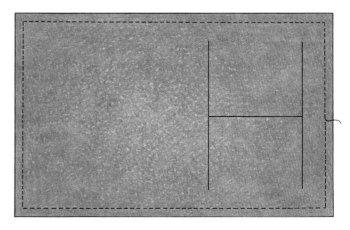

7. Fold back the tabs of the lining leather and place the clear gel skin in position on top. On the gel skin, use a dot to mark the four corners formed by the folded tabs.

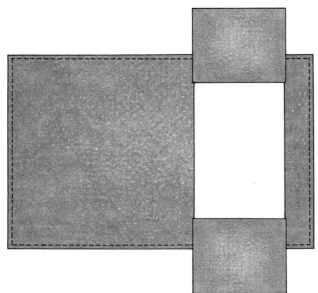

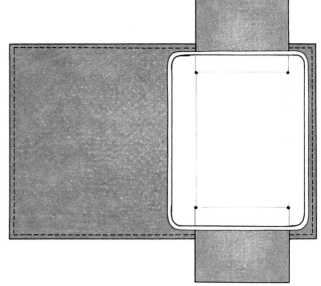

8. Remove the skin and use a snap blade cutter to cut two horizontal lines from dot to dot on the skin.

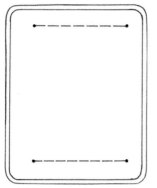

9. Pull the tabs through the cuts in the gel skin. Apply adhesive transfer tape to cover the backs of the tabs. Burnish the tape and peel off the paper backing, and adhere the tabs to the gel skin. Finish the edges of the leather with gum tragacanth or acrylic paint. Insert your e-tablet into the gel skin.

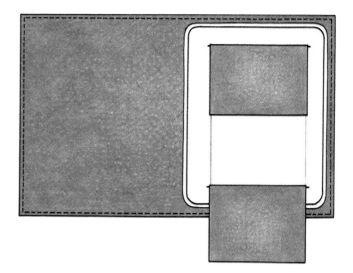

E-Reader Cover

MATERIALS

2 square feet 3-ounce leather for the cover

2 square feet 1-ounce leather for the lining

Clear e-reader gel skin

Plastic or vinyl folder

3½" × 6¼" piece of card stock

3M 465 adhesive transfer tape

Heavy-duty or all-purpose thread

Gum tragacanth or acrylic paint

Masking tape

TOOLS

Sewing machine

Size 14 or 16 leather sewing machine needles

Sewing machine zipper foot

Snap blade cutter

Self-healing cutting mat

Metal straight edge

MAKING THE E-READER COVER

1. Using a snap blade cutter, cutting mat, and straight edge, cut one $9\frac{1}{4}$" × 13" piece from the cover leather and one $9\frac{1}{4}$" × 13" piece from the lining leather.

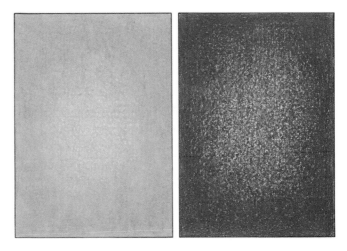

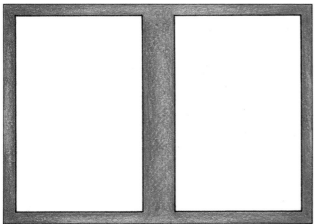

2. Cut two $5\frac{1}{2}$" × $8\frac{1}{4}$" pieces out of the folder. Apply adhesive transfer tape to completely cover the backs of both pieces of plastic. Burnish the tape and peel off the paper backing, and adhere the pieces of plastic to the wrong side of the cover leather $\frac{1}{2}$" from the bottom, top, and sides. The space in the middle will be larger than $\frac{1}{2}$".

3. On the wrong side of the lining leather, place the $3\frac{1}{2}$" × $6\frac{1}{4}$" card $1\frac{1}{2}$" from the top edge and $1\frac{1}{2}$" from the right edge. Trace the two long edges of the card.

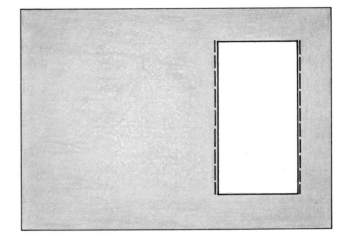

4. Draw a horizontal line to join the mid-points of the two lines, forming an H. Use a snap blade cutter to cut along these lines. This forms the tabs that will hold your gel cover in place.

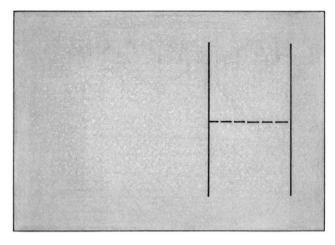

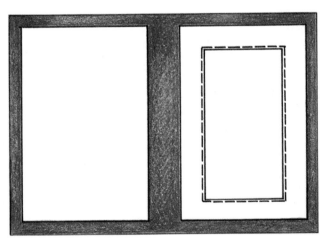

5. Place the 3½" × 6¼" card on the wrong side of the cover leather piece 1½" from the top edge and 1½" from the right edge. Trace around all four sides of the card. Apply adhesive transfer tape to the entire wrong side of the cover leather, except inside this rectangle.

6. Burnish the tape and peel off the paper backing. Adhere the wrong side of the lining leather to the wrong side of the cover leather. (It adds stability if you use masking tape to keep the letter H closed on the right side of the lining leather during this step.) Topstitch around all four sides close to the edge of the plastic (approximately ¼" from the edge). I find it helps to replace your regular sewing machine foot with a zipper foot and use the edge of the foot as a guide for this step. Alternatively, you could move your machine's needle to the far right (if your machine has this option) and use the edge of your regular presser foot as a guide. Use a snap blade cutter to trim the leather ⅛" from the stitching on all four sides.

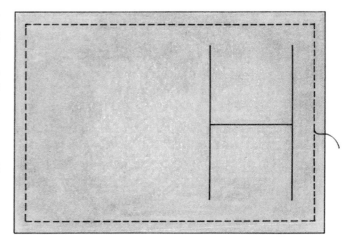

7. Fold back the tabs of the lining leather and place the clear gel skin in position on top. Mark each corner of the rectangle of gel skin between the tabs with a dot.

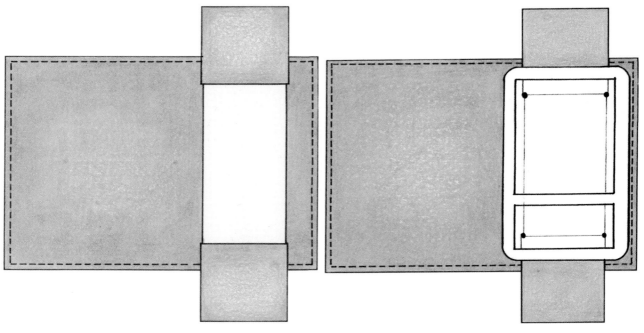

8. Remove the skin and use a snap blade cutter to cut two horizontal lines from dot to dot.

9. Pull the tabs through the cuts in the gel skin. Apply adhesive transfer tape to the backs of the tabs. Burnish the tape and peel off the paper backing, and adhere the tabs to the gel skin. Finish the edges of the leather with gum tragacanth or acrylic paint. Insert your e-reader into the gel skin.

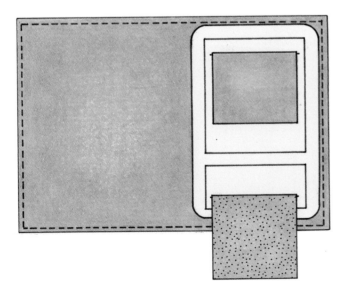

SMARTPHONE COVER

This project is very similar to the e-tablet and e-reader cover projects: The only difference is that it does not have specific measurements, so you can customize it to fit your favorite flavor of phone. You can use every feature on your phone, camera included, while it is in this high-end, luxurious case, and no one will suspect you are sexting.

MATERIALS

½ square foot 3-ounce leather for the cover

½ square foot 1-ounce leather for the lining

Clear gel skin to fit your device

3M 465 adhesive transfer tape

Heavy-duty or all-purpose thread

Gum tragacanth or acrylic paint

Masking tape

TOOLS

Sewing machine

Size 14 or 16 leather sewing machine needles

Snap blade cutter

Self-healing cutting mat

Metal straight edge

MAKING THE SMARTPHONE COVER

1. Put the gel skin on your phone, and place the phone on the right hand side of an 8½" × 11" piece of paper. Draw lines ½" from the phone along the top, bottom, and right side. Draw another line ¾" from the left side of the phone.

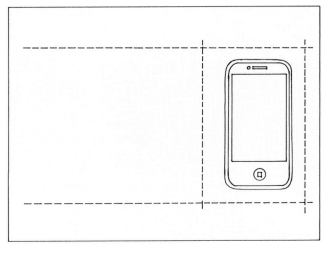

2. Move your phone so that its right edge is along the line drawn farthest left. Draw a line ½" from the phone's left edge. Cut out the larger rectangle formed by these lines. This is your pattern for the outside cover and lining of your phone.

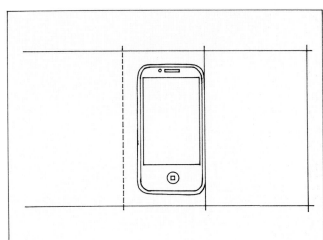

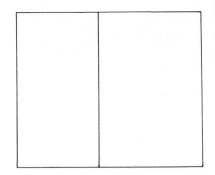

3. Use this pattern and a snap blade cutter, cutting mat, and straight edge to cut one piece from the outside leather and one piece from the lining leather.

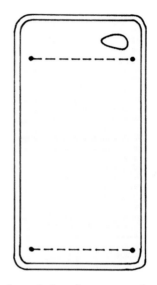

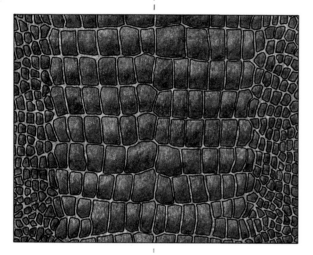

4. Remove the gel skin from your phone. On the back of the gel skin, draw a line parallel to the top, stopping ¼" from each side. If your skin has a camera opening, the line should be ¼" below that opening. Draw another line parallel to the bottom of the gel skin, stopping ¼" from each side. Cut along these lines with a snap blade cutter.

5. With your lining leather piece right side up, place the gel skin ½" from the right, top, and bottom edges. Use a pen to mark a dot at each end of the cut lines in the gel skin. Remove the gel skin and use a pen and straight edge to connect the dots to draw two vertical lines. Draw a horizontal line to join the midpoints of the two lines, forming a letter H. Cut along these lines to form the tabs that hold the gel skin in place.

6. Apply adhesive transfer tape to the entire wrong side of the lining leather, except on the tabs. Burnish the tape and peel off the paper backing, and adhere the wrong side of the lining leather to the wrong side of the cover leather. (It adds stability if you use masking tape to keep the letter H closed on the right side of the lining leather during this step.)

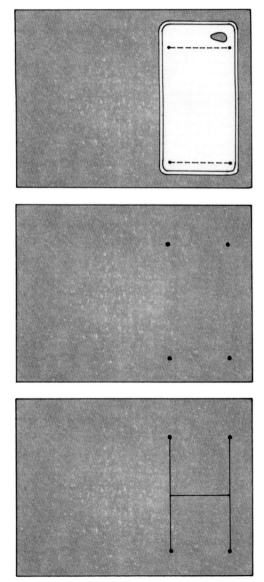

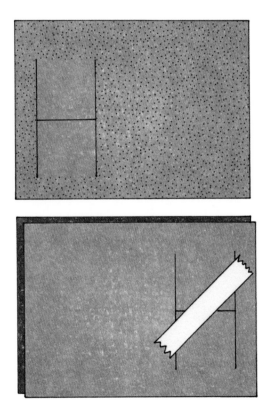

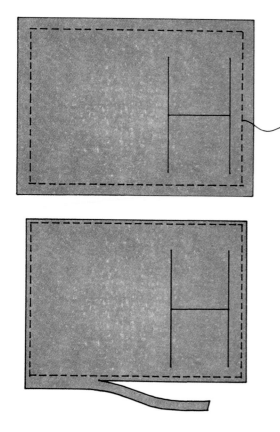

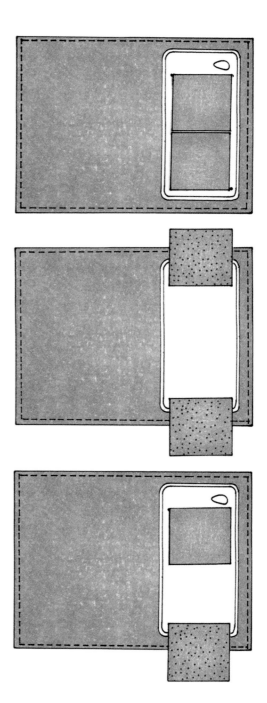

7. Topstitch around all four sides, ¼" from the edge. Use a snap blade cutter and straight edge to trim the leather ⅛" from the stitching on all four sides.

8. Pull the tabs through the cuts in the gel skin. Use a pen to trace the camera hole in your gel skin, remove the skin, and use a snap blade cutter to carefully cut out the camera opening. Replace the skin and apply adhesive transfer tape to the backs of the tabs. Burnish the tape and peel off the paper backing, and adhere the tabs to the gel skin. Finish the edges of the leather with gum tragacanth or acrylic paint. Insert your phone, call your friends, and tell them what a genius you are.

STYLISH

CARRY

ALLS

The bags we carry are our main accessories and there's no denying that women are obsessed with them. This obsession may be for practical reasons—our purses carry around all the odds and ends we need to keep us mobile—but I suspect it is also because as we bounce around from a size 4 to a size 12 to a size 6 to a size 12 and then back down to a size 8, the bag always fits. There is something very stress-free about walking into a store and shopping for a bag. In fact, in the world of fashion, most big designers actually lose money on their clothing lines while their financial success is achieved through the sales of their bags.

It's not just the outside bag that makes the heart go pitter-patter; the bags within the bags, with their singular purpose of organization, are just as well loved. Wallets, makeup cases, and change purses hold just as much appeal as shoulder bags do. If you love the look and feel of high-end bags but are unwilling or unable to blow your entire tax refund check on one, this is the section for you.

SHOPPING TOTE

BYOB used to be code for "a friend is having a party but can't afford to treat everyone to booze." As the world becomes more and more environmentally conscious, the code has shifted to also mean "bring your own bag." The plastic bags handed out so freely at checkout counters can now brand you an environmental pariah, and these days you're expected to have your own means of containment for your organic purchases—or withstand the glares of more righteous shoppers. You can make this tote out of heavy-weight fabric, such as denim or printed canvas, or transform it into something super luxurious by using leather (shown on page 119). Whatever you choose, you're sure to have the best-looking bag in line at Whole Foods.

MATERIALS

1½ yards heavy fabric or
    8 square feet 3-ounce leather
3M 465 adhesive transfer tape
5½" × 13" piece of stiff cardboard
Heavy-duty or all-purpose thread
Gum tragacanth or acrylic paint (if
    using leather)

TOOLS

Sewing machine
Size 14 or 16 leather sewing
    machine needles (if using
    leather)
Snap blade cutter
Self-healing cutting mat
Metal straight edge
Tape measure

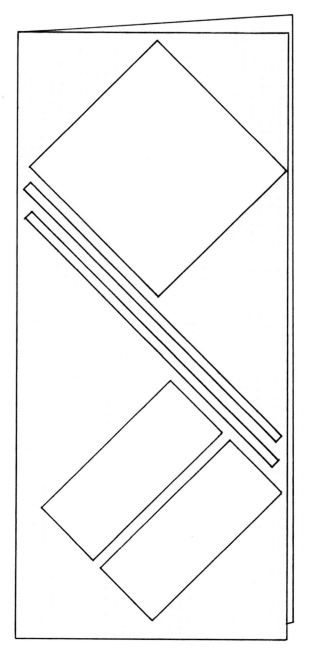

MAKING THE SHOPPING TOTE

1. Using a snap blade cutter, cutting mat, and straight edge, cut from the fabric or leather:

- Four 1" × 22" strips, for the handles
- Two 20" × 20" squares, for the outer bag
- Two 6" × 20" rectangles, for the bag lining
- One 6½" × 14" rectangle, for the bag bottom

2. Apply adhesive transfer tape to completely cover the wrong sides of two of the 1" × 22" handle strips. Burnish the tape and peel off the paper backing, and adhere the strips to the wrong sides of the two remaining handle strips. You should now have two handles made of two layers each. Topstitch each handle ⅛" from each long edge.

Note: All fabric pieces should be cut on the bias.

3. Apply adhesive transfer tape to the last 1" at each end of both handles.

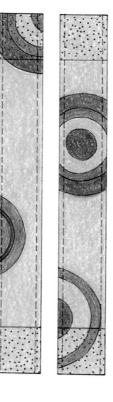

4. On the wrong side of one lining piece, use a pin to mark the center. Repeat with the second lining piece. Then mark 3½" on either side of each center mark. Adhere the handles so that their inside edges align with these outside marks.

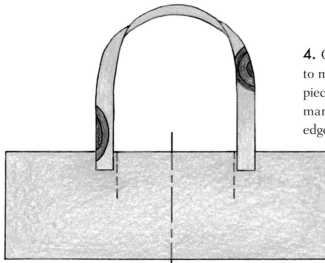

5. Cover the wrong sides of both lining pieces entirely with adhesive transfer tape. Adhere the lining pieces to the outer bag pieces, wrong sides together.

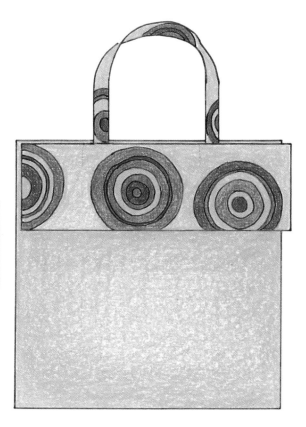

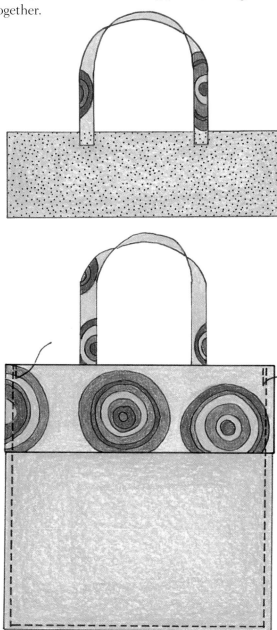

6. Pin the two bag pieces together with right sides facing and sew the sides and bottom of the bag using a ½" seam allowance, back-tacking where you start and end your stitching. You should now be looking at an inside-out bag. Open the seams by pressing them with an iron or by burnishing them. Apply ½" strips of adhesive transfer tape to the wrong sides of the seam allowances. Burnish the tape and peel off the paper backing, and adhere the seam allowances to the inside of the bag to keep them flat and open.

7. Keeping the bag inside out, open one corner so it forms a triangle with the bottom and side seams lined up. Mark a spot 3" down from the end point and draw a line perpendicular to the seam. Sew along this line, back-tacking where you start and finish stitching, and trim the corner off ¼" above the stitch line. Repeat these steps on the opposite corner. Turn the finished bag right side out. If you have made your bag out of leather, finish the edges with gum tragacanth or acrylic paint.

8. To make the bag floor, apply 1" strips of adhesive transfer tape to the edges of the wrong side of the 6½" × 14" piece of fabric or leather. Burnish the tape and peel off the paper backing, and wrap the fabric or leather around the stiff cardboard. Place this floor in the bottom of the bag, leather or fabric side up.

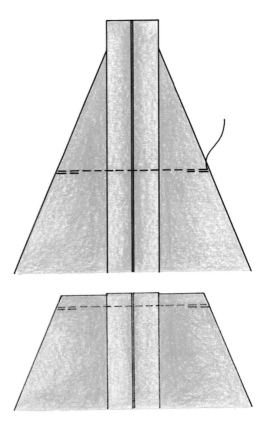

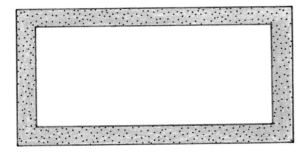

MINK ACROSS-THE-BODY BAG

Big bags are great, but sometimes you just need a little something to hold the essentials, like your keys, cash, and phone. With its across-the-body style, this bag is great for traveling or getting around town. I like to use it as a bag within a bag. Keep it in your larger purse and grab it for a quick getaway. My bag is made with a scrap of mink fur, but it would look just as chic in fabric or leather. I've chosen satin for my lining, but your choices are endless. Just remember that the top of your lining will peek out from inside your bag, so pick something you love. For the purse strap, I've chosen a twisted cord that I purchased from the trimmings department of a fabric store. Again, the options are endless, so think about how you want the colors and textures of the body, lining, and strap to work together.

MATERIALS

Mink fur, fabric, or leather
    (¼ yard, or enough for two
    7" × 8" pieces) for the bag
¼ yard fabric for the lining
1 yard matching cord
All-purpose thread

TOOLS

Sewing machine
Sharp scissors or snap blade
    cutter
Self-healing cutting mat
Metal straight edge
Hand-sewing needle

MAKING THE ACROSS-THE-BODY BAG

1. Using a scissors or snap blade cutter, cutting mat, and straight edge, cut two 7" × 8" pieces of fur, fabric, or leather. If you are using mink, you will want to match the seams in the fur so the stripes line up on the front and back of the bag.

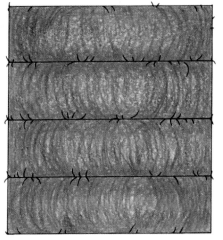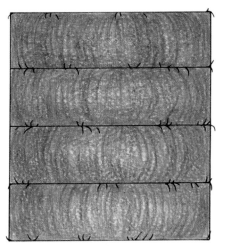

2. Cut two 7" × 9" pieces of lining fabric. (The extra inch will become the contrasting edge that peeks out of the bag.)

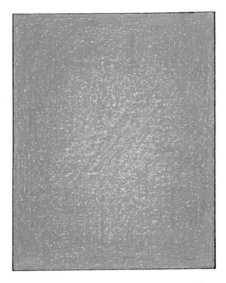

3. Pin the body pieces together with right sides facing. Sew around the sides and bottom using a ¼" seam allowance, back-tacking where you start and finish stitching. Repeat with the lining fabric pieces. Turn only the body of the bag right side out. Use an iron to press the seams of the lining fabric section open.

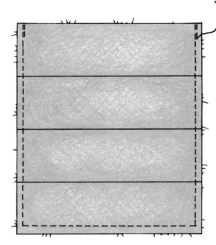

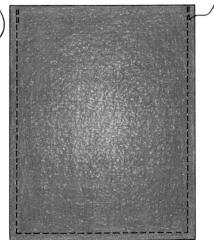

4. Slip the body section into the lining section, lining up the side seams and the top edges of the body and the lining. Pin the pieces together to prevent shifting. Sew along the top, ½" from the edge, leaving a 2" space unsewn in the center of one side. Back-tack where you start and finish stitching.

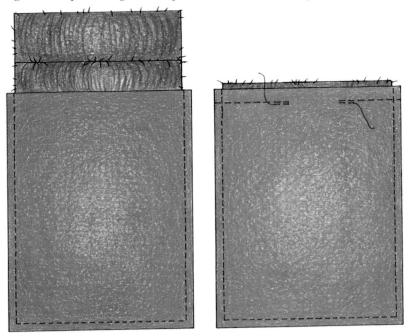

5. Turn the bag right side out through the 2" opening, and tuck the lining fabric into the body of the bag. This will form a ½" border of the lining fabric at the opening of the bag. Press the border down with a warm iron along the top edge.

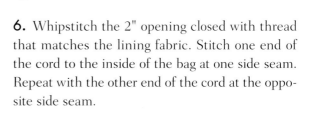

6. Whipstitch the 2" opening closed with thread that matches the lining fabric. Stitch one end of the cord to the inside of the bag at one side seam. Repeat with the other end of the cord at the opposite side seam.

MAN'S BILLFOLD

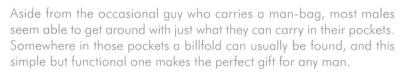

Aside from the occasional guy who carries a man-bag, most males seem able to get around with just what they can carry in their pockets. Somewhere in those pockets a billfold can usually be found, and this simple but functional one makes the perfect gift for any man.

MATERIALS

1 square foot 3-ounce leather

3M 465 adhesive transfer tape

Heavy-duty thread

Gum tragacanth or acrylic paint

TOOLS

Sewing machine

Size 14 or 16 leather sewing
    machine needles

Snap blade cutter

Self-healing cutting mat

Metal straight edge

MAKING THE MAN'S BILLFOLD

1. Use a pen to trace the Men's Billfold Patterns (pages 127–128) onto the wrong side of the leather, and use a snap blade cutter, cutting mat, and straight edge to cut out the pieces. You should have four: two rectangular lining pieces (an inner and an outer one) and two pocket pieces.

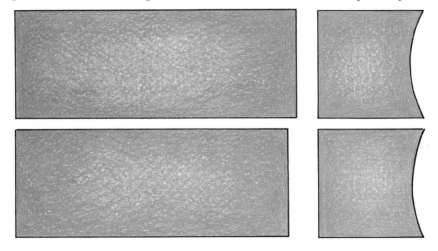

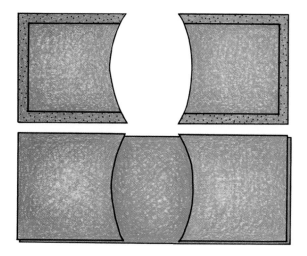

2. Apply ¼" strips of adhesive transfer tape along the straight edges of the wrong sides of the pocket pieces, trimming the tape from the curves as necessary. Burnish the tape and peel off the paper backing. With right sides facing up, adhere the two pocket pieces to the billfold inside piece (the smaller rectangle), lining up the edges and facing the curves toward the center.

3. Stitch along the top edge of each pocket piece. Back-tack where you start and finish stitching.

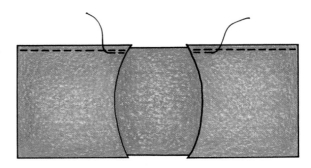

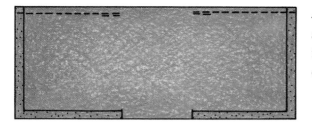

4. Apply ¼" strips of adhesive tape to the ends and bottom edge of the wrong side of the billfold inside piece, stopping where the pocket pieces end.

5. Burnish the tape and peel off the paper backing from the inside piece. Placing wrong sides together, adhere the billfold inside piece to the outside piece, lining up the short ends of both pieces. Your piece will not lie flat when opened because the inside piece is slightly shorter than the outside piece. This will cause a gap in the center, which will allow the billfold to fold flat. Stitch along the sides and bottoms of the pockets, back-tacking where you start and finish stitching.

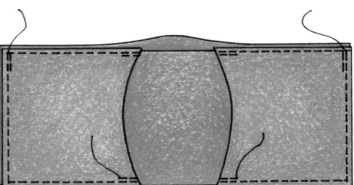

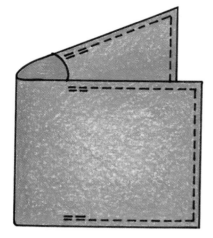

6. Finish the edges of the leather with gum tragacanth or acrylic paint.

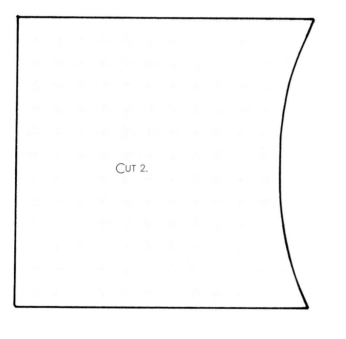

CUT 2.

MAN'S BILLFOLD PATTERN
(shown at 100%)

BILLFOLD OUTSIDE—CUT 1.

BILLFOLD INSIDE—CUT 1.

MAN'S BILLFOLD PATTERN
(shown at 80%)

LARGE MINK HOBO BAG

MATERIALS

Roll of wrapping paper to
    make a pattern
Two 12" × 18" pieces of mink fur
½ yard fabric for the lining
Purchased purse handle,
    approximately 22"
All-purpose thread
Duct tape

TOOLS

Sewing machine
Scissors
Snap blade cutter
Self-healing cutting mat
Metal straight edge
Hand-sewing needle

This glamorous bag is the perfect size for carrying around everything you need on any given day. You can purchase the leather handle at a sewing trimmings or craft store to give it a professional look that will have no one thinking you made it yourself. There is just enough slouch to flash a peek of the lining, so take this opportunity to use a vibrant color and show that you know how to have fun with fashion. Because the dimensions for this bag are large, there is not a pattern in this book, but you can easily make one yourself by following the instructions in step 1. I'm just going to warn you now that one of the ingredients in this stylish recipe is none other than lowly duct tape. Don't judge me.

MAKING THE LARGE MINK HOBO BAG

1. To make the pattern: Use scissors to cut a 12" × 18" piece of paper. Mark a dot 3" up from the bottom on both 12" sides. Mark a dot 1½" in from each edge along the 18" top. Draw a line from the upper dots to the lower dots, and cut along the lines. This is your pattern for the bag.

2. Use this pattern and a snap blade cutter, cutting mat, and straight edge to cut two fur pieces, lining up the fur stripes at the sides. Then use the pattern and a pair of scissors to cut two pieces from your lining fabric.

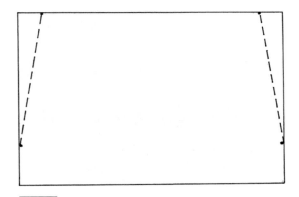

HOBO BAG PATTERN
(shown at 60%)

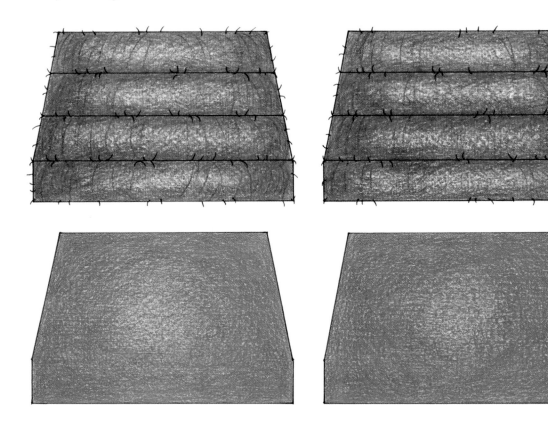

3. Place the two fur pieces with right sides facing, and use a ¼" seam allowance to sew them together along the sides and bottom edges, back-tacking where you start and finish sewing. Repeat with the two lining pieces. Press open the seams of the lining with a warm iron.

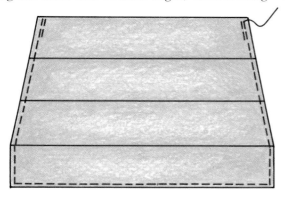

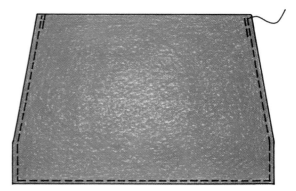

4. To form the bottom of the bag, spread open one inside corner of the fur piece, forming a triangle so that the bottom and side seams line up. Mark a spot 2" in from the point of the triangle and draw a line perpendicular to the seam at that spot. Stitch along this line and trim the fur away ¼" from the stitching. Repeat on the opposite corner of the fur piece and both corners of the lining.

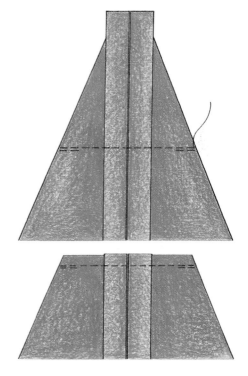

5. Completely cover the floor of the fur piece with three layers of duct tape. Adhere a double layer of duct tape around the top of the fur piece, ¼" from the edge. (This will add body to the bottom and upper edges of the bag.) Turn the fur piece right side out.

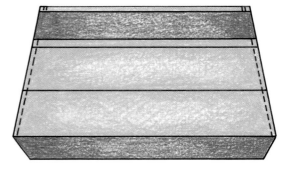

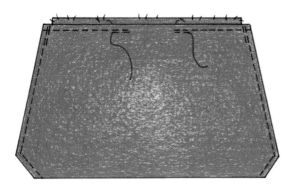

6. Slip the fur piece into the lining piece, matching the side seams and lining up the top edges. (Right sides should be together.) Stitch along the upper edge using a scant ¼" seam allowance to avoid sewing through the duct tape. Leave a 4" opening in the center. Back-tack where you start and finish stitching.

7. Turn the bag right side out through the opening and tuck the lining into the fur bag. Hand stitch the handle into the lining of the bag at the side seams.

DROP LOCK WALLET

The wallet is undoubtedly the most important item in any purse, and it deserves as much consideration as the purse itself. This stylish wallet not only has a place to securely carry your debit card (my personal lifeline) but it expands to become roomy enough to hold a cell phone, keys, and lip gloss as well as double as a clutch.

MATERIALS

2 square feet 3-ounce leather (you'll need two 8" × 12" pieces)

Drop lock hardware

3M 465 adhesive transfer tape

Heavy-duty thread

Gum tragacanth or acrylic paint

TOOLS

Sewing machine

Size 14 or 16 leather sewing machine needles

Snap blade cutter

Self-healing cutting mat

Metal straight edge

Credit card

Small screwdriver

MAKING THE DROP LOCK WALLET

1. Use the snap blade cutter, cutting mat, and straight edge to cut two 8" × 12" pieces of leather. On the wrong side of each piece, place a credit card ¼" from one 8" edge (this will be the top) and ¼" from the right edge and trace around the perimeter. Trace again ¼" from the top and ¼" from the left edge.

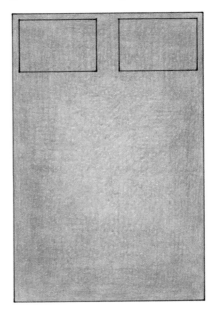

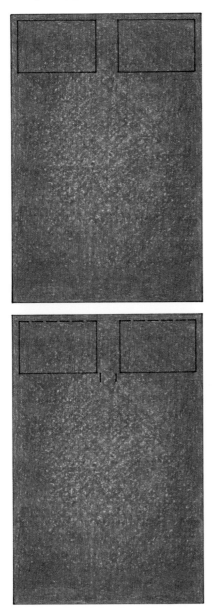

2. On a piece of leather to be the outside of the wallet, cut along the top of the credit card lines with the snap blade cutter. Place the latch portion of the drop lock hardware in the center, with the top of the latch aligned with the bottoms of the credit card tracings. Mark the cut lines for the prongs.

3. Turn the leather right side up and install the latch. (This will be the outside of the wallet.)

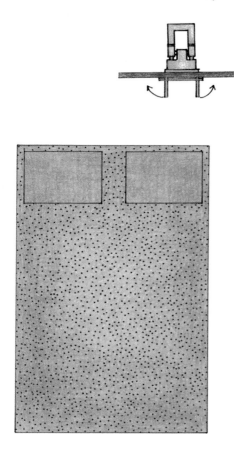

4. Apply adhesive transfer tape to the wrong side of the second piece of leather, completely covering everywhere except inside the credit card tracings. (This will be the lining of the wallet.)

5. Burnish the tape and peel off the paper backing. With wrong sides together, adhere the lining piece to the wrong side of the outer piece, carefully lining up the edges.

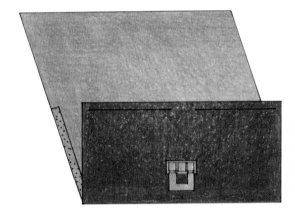

6. Directly below the hardware, fold back what will be the credit card slot portion of the wallet, leaving a 4" flap. Adhere the sides of the folded portion with ¼" strips of adhesive transfer tape.

7. Topstitch ⅛" from the edge of one side of the wallet, beginning at the bottom and back-tacking when you reach the raw edge. Repeat on the opposite side of the wallet. Topstitch around the top of the wallet, back-tacking where the wallet body meets the flap.

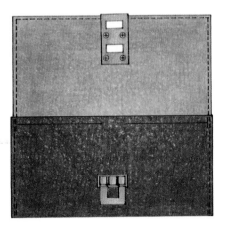

8. Follow the instructions to install the drop lock hardware (pages 53 to 54) to attach the slot portion to the center of the flap. Finish the edges of the leather with gum tragacanth or acrylic paint.

BELTED WALLET

The size and construction of this chic wallet is much the same as the Drop Lock Wallet, but taking the time to add the extra detail of the strap and hardware gives you a high-end look at a homemade price.

MATERIALS

2 square feet 3-ounce leather (you'll need two 8" × 12" pieces and two ⅝" × 18½" strips)

1" strap loop

Two 1" snap hooks

3M 465 adhesive transfer tape

Heavy-duty thread

Gum tragacanth or acrylic paint

TOOLS

Sewing machine

Size 14 or 16 leather sewing machine needles

Snap blade cutter

Self-healing cutting mat

Metal straight edge

Credit card

Small screwdriver

MAKING THE BELTED WALLET

1. Use the snap blade cutter, cutting mat, and straight edge to cut two pieces of leather 8" × 12". On the wrong side of each piece, place a credit card ¼" from one 8" edge (this will be the top) and ¼" from the right edge and trace around the perimeter. Trace again ¼" from the top and ¼" from the left edge.

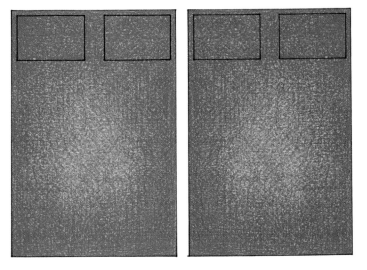

2. On the piece of leather to be the outside of the wallet, cut along the top of the credit card lines with the snap blade cutter.

3. Apply the strap loop hardware to the bottom center of the outer wallet ¾" up from the edge.

4. Apply adhesive transfer tape to the wrong side of the second piece of leather, completely covering everywhere except inside the credit card tracings. (This will be the lining piece of the wallet.)

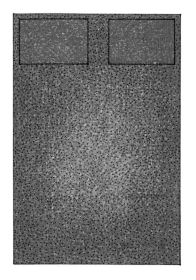

5. With wrong sides together, adhere the lining piece to the wrong side of the outer piece, carefully lining up the edges.

6. Directly below the hardware, fold back what will be the credit card slot portion of the wallet, leaving a 4" flap. Adhere the sides of the folded portion with ¼" strips of adhesive transfer tape.

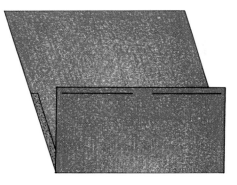

7. Topstitch ⅛" from the edge of the sides and top of the wallet. Back-tack where the wallet body meets the flap.

8. Cut one strip of leather ½" × 14½" and one ½" × 12½". Completely cover the wrong side of the short strip with adhesive transfer tape. Burnish the tape and peel off the paper backing and adhere the two strips together. Topstitich ⅛" from the edge along both lengths. Fold the ends of the stitched strap through the loops of the snap hooks. Sew across and back-tack all stitches.

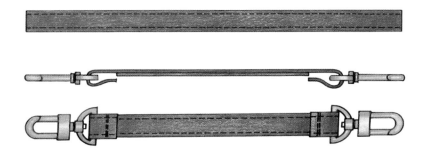

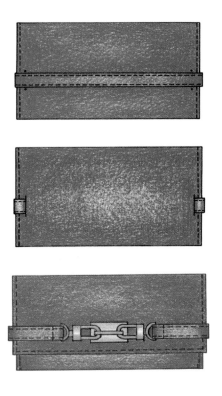

9. Connect the hooks to the strap loop. Turn the wallet over and make sure the strap is parallel to the top and bottom edges of the wallet before you use a sharp pencil to make small dots directly over and under the strap, ½" from the edges of the wallet. Remove the strap and place the corner of a self-healing mat inside the wallet before using a snap blade cutter and straight edge to cut from each upper to lower dot.

10. From the inside of the wallet, push each strap end through these cuts and wrap the strap around the front of the wallet to meet the circle lock. Finish the edges of the leather with gum tragacanth or acrylic paint.

LEATHER DAY CLUTCH

This little curved clutch is a purse and a wallet all in one. It has compartments for all the essentials and comfortably holds credit cards, cash, a phone, and keys, so it's perfect for running quick errands. Leave it in your big bag and grab it when just a little something will do.

MATERIALS

3 square feet 3-ounce leather

Twist-lock hardware

3M 465 adhesive transfer tape

Heavy-duty or all-purpose thread

Gum tragacanth or acrylic paint

TOOLS

Sewing machine

Size 14 or 16 leather sewing machine needles

Snap blade cutter

Self-healing cutting mat

Metal straight edge

Credit card

Small binder clips

Small screwdriver

MAKING THE LEATHER DAY CLUTCH

1. Use a snap blade cutter, cutting mat, and straight edge to cut two pieces of leather 9" × 13½". On the wrong side of one of the pieces, place a credit card ½" from one 9" edge (this will be the top) and ¾" from the right edge, and trace around the perimeter. Trace the card again ¾" from the left side.

2. Use a snap blade cutter and a straight edge to cut along the tops of the credit card tracings. Using the turn portion of the turn-lock hardware, mark and cut lines for the prongs in the center, 3" down from the top edge.

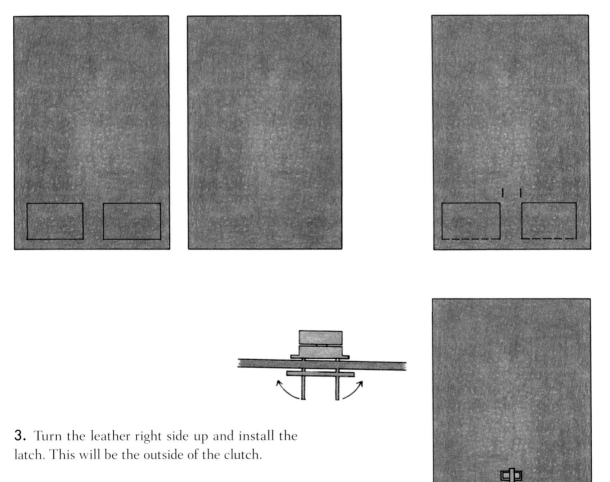

3. Turn the leather right side up and install the latch. This will be the outside of the clutch.

4. On the wrong side of the second piece of leather, draw a line 8" up from one shorter edge and ¼" from the right edge. Repeat on the left side and cut away these sections with a snap blade cutter. This will be the lining of the clutch.

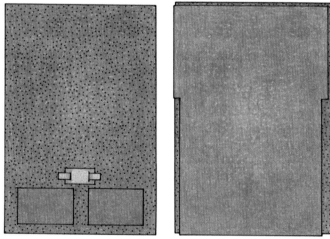

5. Apply adhesive transfer tape to the entire wrong side of the outer piece, except for inside the credit card tracings. Burnish the tape and peel off the paper backing. With wrong sides together and the narrower end of the lining covering the backs of the credit card slots, adhere the outer piece to the lining piece. Two ¼" × 8" strips of adhesive will be exposed.

6. Using the Side Gusset Pattern (see page 145), cut two gusset pieces from the leather. With wrong sides together, adhere the gusset pieces to the exposed strip of adhesive on the clutch body.

7. Because the adhesive strip is so narrow, use small binder clips to hold the pieces together while you sew. With the gusset side up, stitch along the gusset pieces ⅛" from the edge to form the sides of the clutch. Back-tack where you start and finish stitching. This step is a bit tricky, but matching your thread and leather colors will help hide crafts-manship issues and using your machine's free arm will make it easier to perform this step.

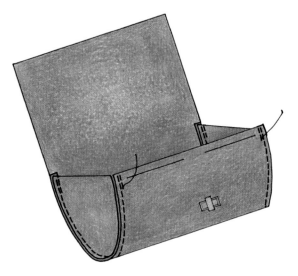

8. Mark the center of the inner lining flap, place the bottom of the eyelet plate ⅜" from the edge, and trace the opening. Remove the plate and use a snap blade cutter to cut out the opening. Install the hardware, using a small screwdriver to connect the bottom plate to the top plate. Use the corner curve template to mark and trim the flap corners. Finish the edges of the leather with gum tragacanth or acrylic paint.

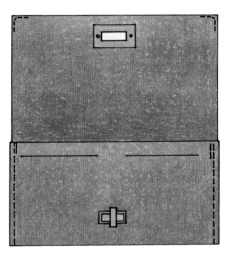

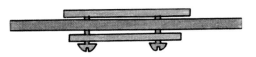

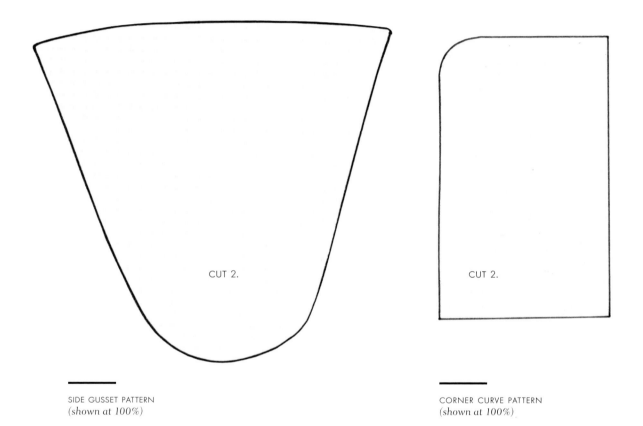

CUT 2.

CUT 2.

SIDE GUSSET PATTERN
(shown at 100%)

CORNER CURVE PATTERN
(shown at 100%)

ELEGANT BACKPACK

MATERIALS

3 square feet 3-ounce leather for the pack

1 square foot 1-ounce leather for the lining

4" × 8" piece of noncorrugated, stiff cardboard

3M 465 adhesive transfer tape

Heavy-duty or all-purpose thread

Gum tragacanth or acrylic paint

This design came about after I realized that herding small children through the streets of New York is not easy and that it helps to have your hands free while trying to maneuver an infant in her stroller down the subway stairs. A backpack is a perfect solution. However, my quest for a backpack only turned up sporty styles, and it's hard to pull off a Patagonia pack when you're wearing stilettos. So I decided to make my own. This simplified version of a sporty backpack doesn't feature 15 zippered compartments or a net to hold a water bottle, but it certainly holds a couple of baby bottles and enough diapers to get you through the day, with room left over for some informative reading material.

TOOLS

Sewing machine

Size 14 or 16 leather sewing machine needles

Snap blade cutter

Self-healing cutting mat

Metal straight edge

Small metal binder clips

MAKING THE ELEGANT BACKPACK

1. Use a snap blade cutter, cutting mat, and straight edge to cut two 9½" × 9½" pieces from the backpack leather and two 9½" × 4" pieces from the lining leather. Using the Backpack Bottom Pattern (see page 159), cut out one oval from the backpack leather. You should now have five pieces: two square outer body pieces, two rectangular lining pieces, and an oval for the bottom.

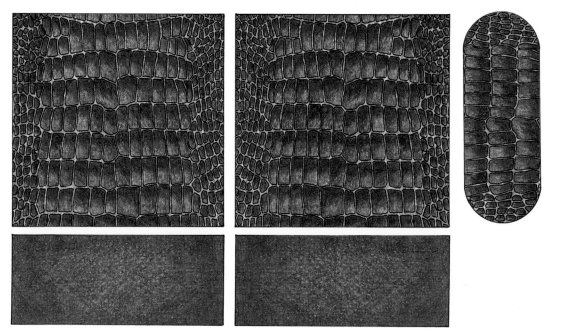

2. Cut four strips of the backpack leather, each ½" × 33". Apply adhesive transfer tape to the wrong side of one of the strips. With wrong sides together, adhere that strip to another strip. Repeat with the remaining two strips, forming two 33" straps.

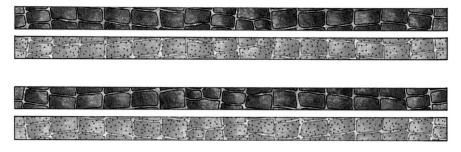

3. Cut a strip of backpack leather ½" × 5½". Apply adhesive transfer tape to the wrong side of the strip and fold the strip in half lengthwise. Stitch ⅛" from the raw edge. Trim strip close to stitching. This strip will form a loop for the straps to run through.

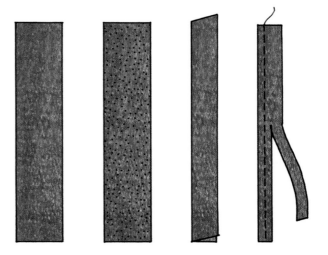

4. Use adhesive transfer tape to completely cover 1" at one end of each 33" strap. Burnish the tape and peel off the paper backing. Adhere the straps to the center top of the wrong side of the front body piece, leaving a ½" space between the straps. Apply 1" of adhesive transfer tape to each end of the 5½" strip. Adhere it to the center of the back body piece to form a loop with a 1½" space inside.

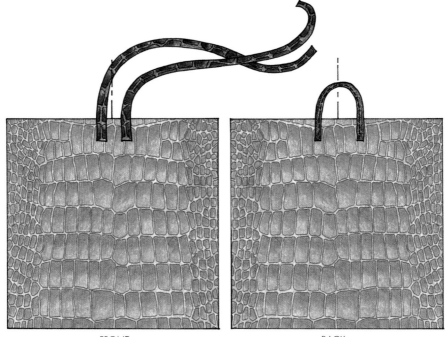

FRONT   BACK

5. Entirely cover the wrong sides of both lining pieces with adhesive transfer tape. Burnish the tape and peel off the paper backing. Adhere the lining pieces to the wrong sides of the front and back pieces, aligning the edges of the leather and covering the raw ends of the straps and loop. Topstitch ⅛" from the edge of both pieces.

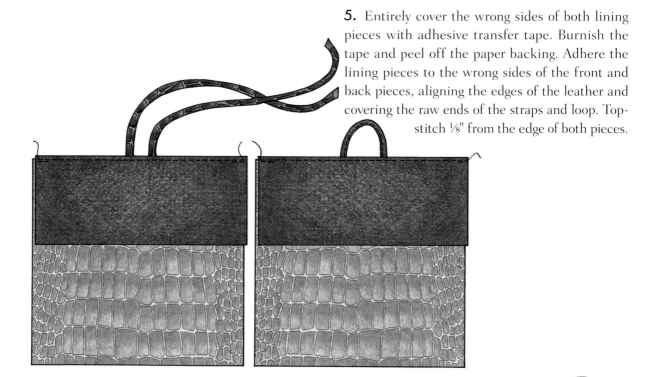

6. Apply ¼" strips of adhesive transfer tape along the long edges on the wrong sides of one of the front pieces. Burnish the tape and peel off the paper backing. Adhere the front piece to the back piece. Topstitch ⅛" from the edge on each side, back-tacking where you start and finish stitching.

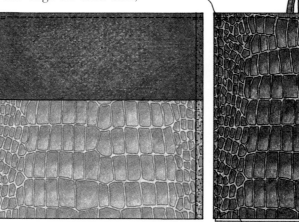

7. Slip the strap ends through the loop on the back body piece and apply adhesive transfer tape to the bottom 1" of the straps. Burnish the tape and peel off the paper backing. Adhere the strap ends to the very center of the wrong side of the oval bottom piece.

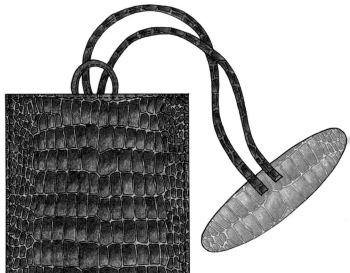

8. Turn the bag body inside out, and with right sides together, secure the oval bottom piece in place with small binder clips, lining up the center points of the short ends of the oval with the body side seams. Make sure your straps aren't twisted, and stitch the bottom oval to the bag body ⅛" from the edge, back-tacking where you start and finish stitching.

9. Turn the bag right side out. Using the Equestrian Bag Pattern (see page 159), cut an oval of stiff cardboard. Trim ¼" around the edge and place the bottom in the bag. Finish the edges of the leather with gum tragacanth or acrylic paint.

EQUESTRIAN BAG

MATERIALS

6 square feet 3-ounce leather for the bag

2 square feet 1-ounce leather for the lining

1" strap loop

Two 1" snap hooks

Two 1¼" split D rings

Two ¼" leather studs

3M 465 adhesive transfer tape

Heavy-duty thread

Gum tragacanth or acrylic paint

TOOLS

Sewing machine

Size 14 or 16 leather sewing machine needles

Small metal binder clips

Snap blade cutter

Self-healing cutting mat

Metal straight edge

Small screwdriver

Leather hole punch

Pliers

Reminiscent of the type of bag used to feed New York City carriage horses, this casual purse is perfect for everyday use. The strap is long enough to wear messenger style and the hardware keeps the bag securely closed. I warn you that this is perhaps the most advanced project in the book, not because any single step is difficult but because it incorporates so many design elements from other projects. If you have tried your hand at some of the smaller projects in the previous sections, this one should be no problem for you. You can also make this bag out of denim, canvas, or Ultrasuede.

MAKING THE EQUESTRIAN BAG

1. Use a snap blade cutter, cutting mat, and straight edge to cut two 14¾" × 14½" pieces of the bag leather. Because the two measurements are so similar, mark a T (for top) on the wrong side of one 14¾" edge, but on both pieces. These pieces will be the outer bag front and back.

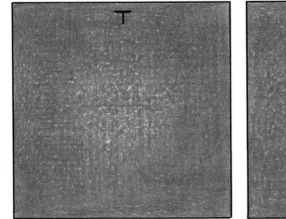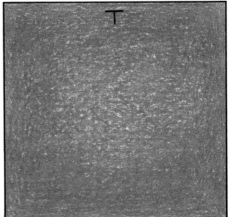

2. Use the Bottom Pattern (see page 159) to cut two ovals from the bag leather. Trim ¼" from the edge of one of the ovals. This smaller oval will be the inside floor of the bag, while the untrimmed piece will be the outer bag bottom.

3. Cut two 1" × 36" strips from the bag leather.

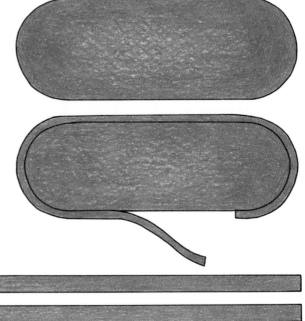

4. Install the strap loop hardware to the center of the outer bag front ¾" from the top edge. Mark the placement of the prongs and cut with a snap blade cutter. Insert the prongs, slip on the backplate, and fold the prongs outward.

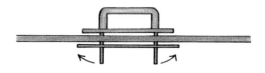

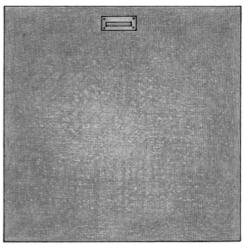

5. Apply adhesive transfer tape to the wrong sides of both lining pieces. Adhere the lining pieces to the wrong sides of the body pieces, lining up the top and side edges. Topstitch along the top edges ⅛" from the edge.

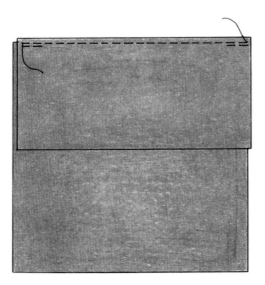

6. Apply ¼" strips of adhesive transfer tape to the entire length of the side edges of the back body piece. Burnish the tape and peel off the paper backing. With wrong sides facing, adhere the front body piece to the back body piece. Stitch along the sides of the bag ⅛" from the edge. Back-tack where you start and finish stitching.

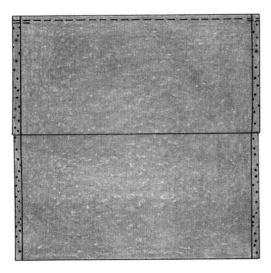

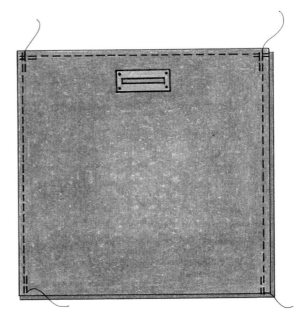

7. Place the bag body flat and use the Equestrian Bag Slot Template (see page 158) to mark the slot positions. Cut the slots through all four layers of the lining and outer bag leather.

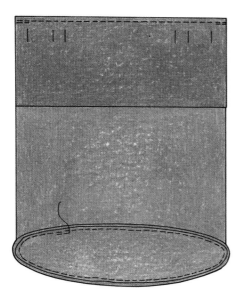

8. Turn the bag body inside out, and with right sides together, secure the larger oval bottom piece in place with small binder clips, lining up the center points of the short ends of the oval with the body side seams. Stitch the bottom oval to the bag body ⅛" from the edge.

9. Cut one ½" × 19" and one ½" × 17" strip from the body leather. Apply adhesive transfer tape to the wrong side of the shorter strip. Burnish, peel, and adhere the two strips. Topstitch ⅛" from the edge along both edges. Fold the ends of the strap through the loops of the snap hooks. Sew across and back-tack all stitches. Weave the strap through the slots.

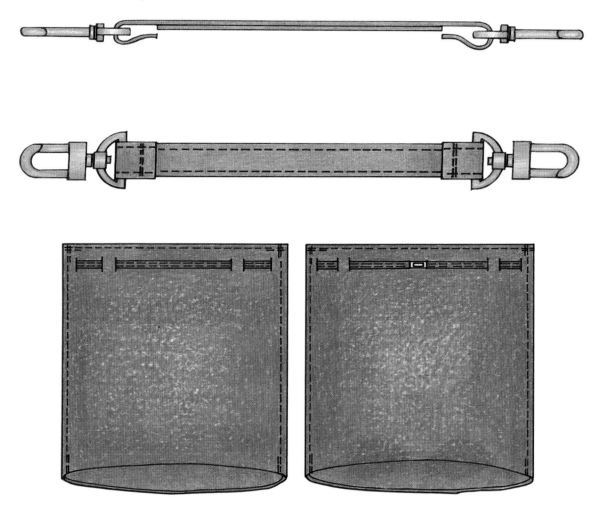

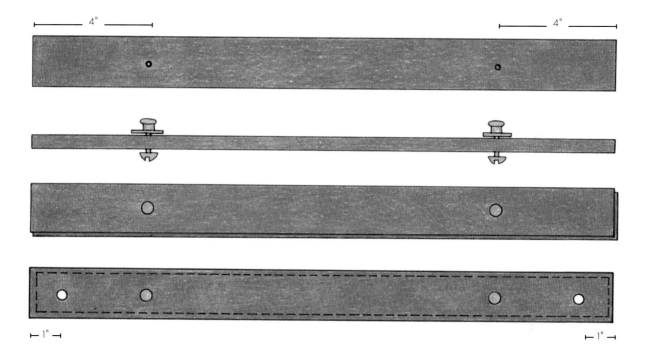

10. Use the leather hole punch to punch a ³⁄₁₆" hole 4" from each end of one of the 1" × 36" leather straps you cut in step 3. Insert the leather studs and secure them with the provided screw on the wrong side of the leather. Apply adhesive transfer tape to the wrong side of the other strap. With wrong sides together, adhere the two strap pieces. Stitch ⅛" from the edge around all four sides of the strap.

11. In the upper left and right hand corners of the front of the bag, make a dot ½" from the top edge and ½" from the side edge. Use the leather hole punch to punch a ³⁄₁₆" hole in each spot. Insert the split D rings. You may need to use a pair of pliers to twist the D ring open and form a gap large enough to slip it through the punched hole. Gently squeeze the ring closed after you have slipped it through the hole. Turn the rings so that the flat sides are facing up and insert the strap ends with the studs facing out. Punch a ³⁄₁₆" hole 1" from each end of the strap and push the studs through the holes. Finish the edges of the leather with gum tragacanth or acrylic paint.

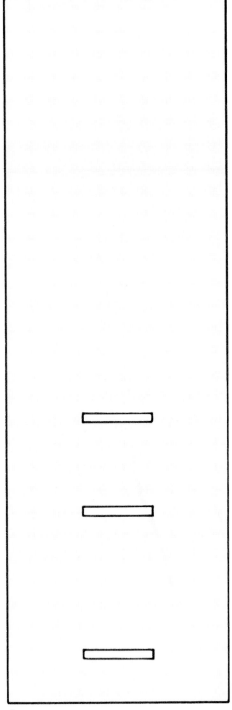

EQUESTRIAN BAG SLOT TEMPLATE
(half template shown at 100%)

PLACE ALONG TOP EDGE.

PLACE ALONGSIDE EDGE.

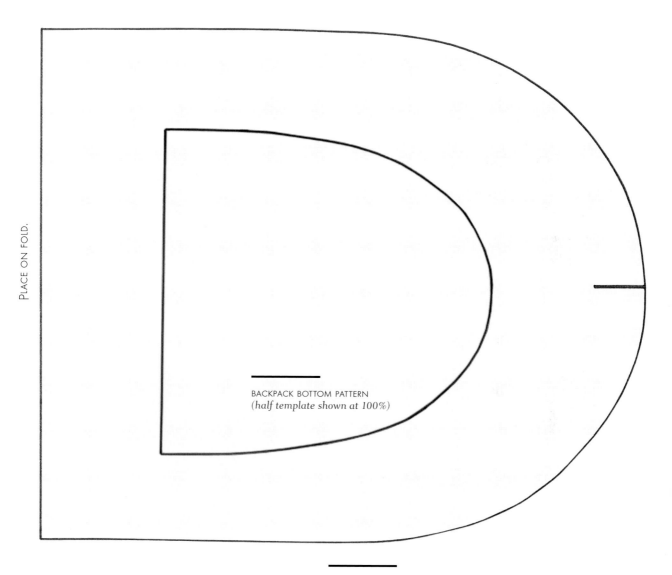

PLACE ON FOLD.

BACKPACK BOTTOM PATTERN
(half template shown at 100%)

EQUESTRIAN BAG BOTTOM TEMPLATE
(half template shown at 100%)

EVENING
EXTRAVA

GANCES

Because they are often used only for special occasions and don't see as much wear and tear as everyday clothes, evening accessories are the treasures that seem most often to be handed down from mothers to daughters. The dresses, bags, and shoes in this section will accompany you to major life events—weddings, graduations, and awards banquets—but because I believe that every day is a day to celebrate, this section includes pieces that will make even a quiet evening at home feel extravagant.

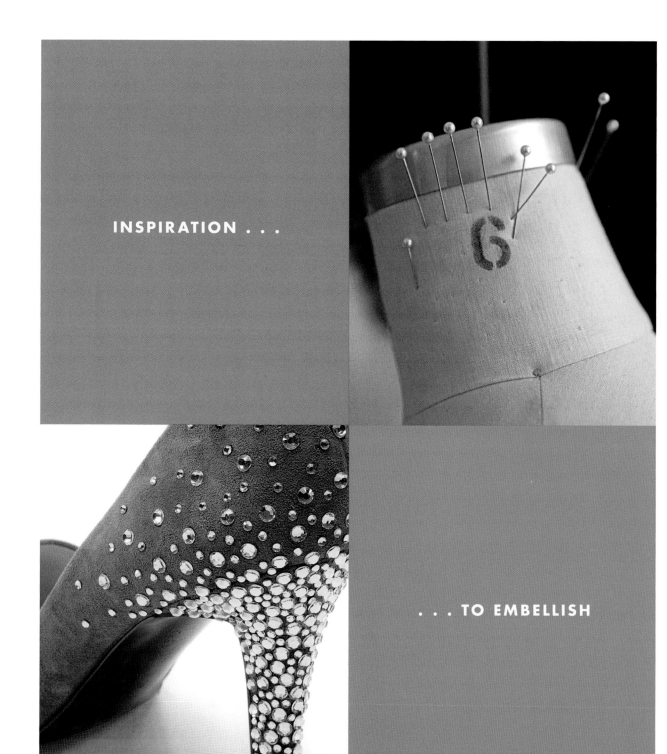

INSPIRATION . . .

. . . TO EMBELLISH

FADE-OUT BEADED DRESS

Buy a simple dress in the silhouette that flatters you most (or use one you already have in your closet) and use this technique to add instant fabulous. For the best results, look for a dress with fabric that has a bit of body so it can handle the weight of the stones and beads. A fabric that is too flimsy may hang improperly after embellishment. The secret to this technique is marking and applying the rhinestones in zones—it's so easy you simply can't make a mistake. It looks great done in a tone-on-tone scheme or in a contrasting color. Adding dark-colored beads to the waist of a light-colored dress delivers an instant minimizing effect due to the play of dark against light. I'm high-waisted, so I use this technique to visually lower my waistline. Who knew that these spectacular gems could be so practical?

MATERIALS

Dress

6 gross ss10 hot-fix rhinestones

4 gross ss16 hot-fix rhinestones

2 gross ss20 hot-fix rhinestones

Accent beads or sequins (optional)

All-purpose thread

TOOLS

Hand-sewing needle small enough to fit through your beads

Iron

Tailor's chalk or pins

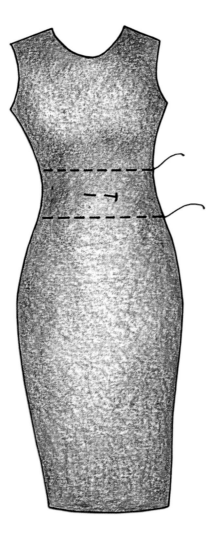

MAKING THE FADE-OUT BEADED DRESS

1. Use tailor's chalk or pins to mark the waistline of the dress to be beaded. Using a needle and thread, baste two lines around the entire garment: one 1½" above the waistline and one 1½" below the waistline. The area between these two basted lines is zone 1.

2. Baste a line 2" above the top line of zone 1 and a line 2" below the bottom line of zone 1. The area between these two lines is zone 2. Baste additional lines 2" above and below the lines that mark zone 2. The area between these two basted lines is zone 3. Note that zone 2 includes all of zone 1, and zone 3 includes all of zones 1 and 2.

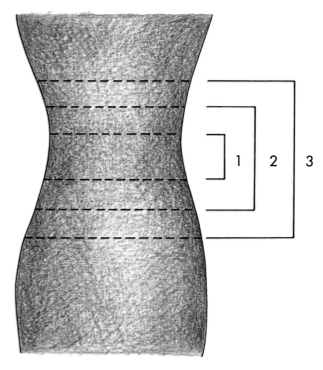

3. Use my "scatter and turn" method (page 16) to evenly distribute the smallest rhinestones (ss10) throughout zone 3. The stones should be approximately ¾" to 1" apart. Follow the instructions in Applying Hot-Fix Rhinestones (page 16) to iron on all of the stones in zone 3.

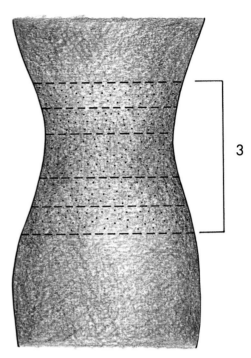

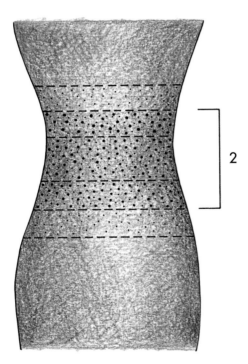

4. Distribute the medium-size rhinestones (ss16) evenly throughout zone 2. The stones in this zone should be approximately ½" apart. Iron on all of the stones in zone 2.

5. Distribute the largest stones (ss20) in zone 1. These stones should be rather dense, about ¼" apart. Iron on all of the stones in zone 1.

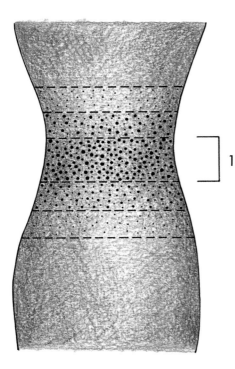

6. For extra sparkle, I often add some novelty beads or sequins that coordinate with the colors of the rhinestones I applied in zone 1. If you want to add any special beads or sequins, be sure to sew them on and knot them individually. It takes a bit more time, but running a stitch from bead to bead without knotting in between almost always leads to an avalanche of beads falling onto the dance floor.

Note: This zoning technique also works well when you're embellishing the hem of a garment. When marking the zones for a hem, zone 1 should be at the bottom, and you need to baste only the upper parts of zones 2 and 3.

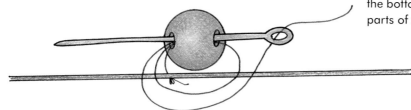

EMBELLISHED SHOES

I see almost everything as a blank canvas begging for a bit of sparkle, and plain shoes are no exception. A simple pair of satin pumps, stilettos, or flats is a perfect place to add high-fashion flair. Don't hate those old bridesmaid heels in the back of your closet; get out the hot-fix rhinestones and transform them into something fabulous. The sizes of rhinestones I recommend here are just that: recommendations. This is actually the perfect project for using up leftover stones from previous projects, so see what you have before you go shopping for new sparkle.

MATERIALS

Pair of shoes
1 gross ss10 hot-fix rhinestones
1 gross ss16 hot-fix rhinestone
1 gross ss20 hot-fix rhinestones

TOOLS

Beeswax
Two bamboo skewers
Adhesive (I recommend Beacon 527 Multi-Use Glue)

MAKING THE EMBELLISHED SHOES

1. Place a small ball of beeswax on one end of a bamboo skewer. You will use this skewer to pick up stones and the other skewer to position and release the stones.

2. Place an assortment of stones right side up on your work surface.

3. To completely cover an area, spread glue over a ½" × ½" area on the shoe. Using the skewer with the ball of wax, pick up the stones one by one and place them in the glue. Use the second skewer to help release the stone from the wax. Use a variety of sizes to fill in the space. Avoid putting too many stones of like sizes together or placing stones in obvious rows. The idea is to make the arrangement look random, not like a pattern. When you've filled in that area, spread glue over an adjacent area and repeat the process.

4. To apply the stones in a fade-out pattern, put a small puddle of glue on a disposable surface, such as a paper plate or a piece of foil. Using the waxed skewer, pick up a large stone and dip the wrong side in the glue. Place the stone on the lowest portion of the shoe and use the second skewer to help release the stone from the wax. Form the fade-out design by applying more large stones in the lowest portion of the area to be embellished. Intersperse with medium-size stones, and finish with the smallest stones near the top of the shoe.

5. Refresh your glue often. The surface of glue tends to skim over after 10 minutes, making it difficult to dip stones, so this simple step will save you time and aggravation.

MINK SWEATER

This chic fur top is not only easy to wear with both jeans and skirts, but it's also surprisingly easy to make. All you have to do is sew together four modified squares. Of course, you can always use a good quality faux fur, but I can't think of a better way to reuse a granny stole or an old mink coat. I make mine out of long rectangular vintage stoles that I buy on eBay, usually for about $99, but I have paid as much as $150 for one in a more unusual color, such as white or silver. Look for straight stoles that are about 80 inches long and 12 to 14 inches wide. The width of the stole will determine the length of the top you can make from it. You can also make this top using the bottom portion of a coat, and if you do so you'll have plenty of fur left over for smaller projects. I have chosen to line my top with satin, but a cute cotton print would work just as well and give this project a totally different feel. My directions also call for grosgrain ribbon, but any kind will do. The pattern directions given here will make a medium-size top that will fit up to a size 40 bust, but you can always make the pattern larger or smaller by adding or deleting from the center front and back. Because this top is so quick to put together, you may want to sew one up in muslin or scrap fabric to check for fit before you cut into your fur.

MATERIALS

Roll of kraft paper
    for the pattern
Rectangular mink stole or 1 yard
    60"-wide faux mink fur
1 yard satin fabric
3 yards 1" grosgrain ribbon
All-purpose thread

TOOLS

Sewing machine
Sharp scissors or snap blade
    cutter
Self-healing cutting mat
Metal straight edge
Iron
Hand-sewing needles

MAKING THE MINK SWEATER

1. Cut a 20" × 22" rectangle from the kraft paper. Draw a horizontal line through the center of the rectangle. This line marks the bottom of the sleeve opening.

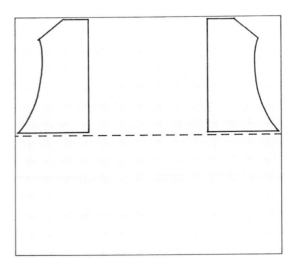

2. Place the Arm Opening Pattern (see page 177) on the far left side of the paper, lining up the top of the pattern with the top of the paper and the bottom of the pattern on the horizontal line you drew in step 1. Trace the pattern onto the paper. Flip the pattern over and place it on the far right side of the paper, tracing to create a mirror image of the left side. Use scissors to cut along the outer edges. This is the paper pattern for the front and back body pieces. Repeat steps 1 and 2 to make a second paper body pattern piece.

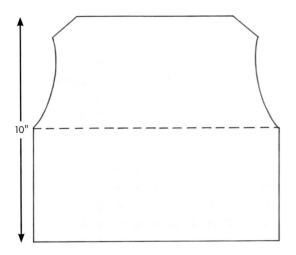

3. Measure and cut a 13¾" × 14" rectangle from the kraft paper. Fold the paper in half lengthwise and place the Sleeve Pattern (see page 176) at the top, lining up the side indicated on the pattern with the fold. Trace the pattern and cut through both layers of paper along the curved line to make one sleeve. Repeat to make the second sleeve.

4. Fold the stole in half and mark the center with a pin. Working from the center out, place the paper sleeve and body pattern pieces on the wrong side of the stole, and trace around them. Your pattern pieces will be longer than the stole. Cut out the pieces with scissors or a snap blade cutter, being careful to cut the leather only, not the hairs.

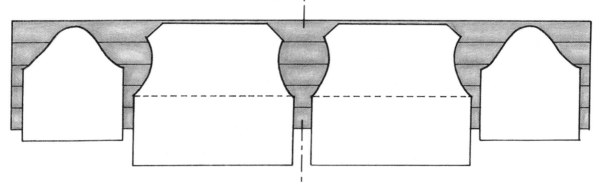

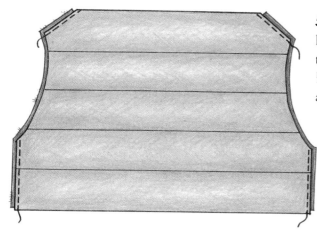

5. With right sides together and the fur stripes lined up, pin the back and front body pieces together. Sew the shoulder and side seams using a ⅛" seam allowance, back-tacking where you start and finish sewing.

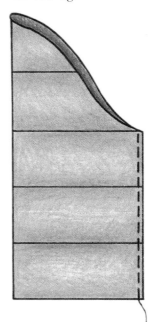

6. Fold both sleeve pieces with their right sides together, lining up and pinning the edges. Sew the sleeve seams, using a ⅛" seam allowance.

7. Turn the sleeves right side out. With the shoulder curve up and the wrist opening down, insert a sleeve into the body piece and pin it into the sleeve opening, matching the center top with the shoulder seams and the sleeve seams with the body side seams. Stitch using a ⅛" seam allowance.

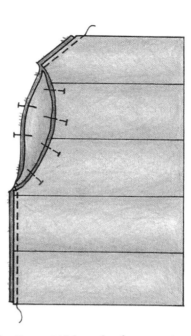

8. Cut a 32" length of grosgrain ribbon. Turn the top right side out and pin the grosgrain ribbon around the neck opening, carefully aligning the edges. Sew the ribbon to the top using a ⅛" seam allowance. Do the same to the bottom of the shirt and the sleeve openings. (This creates a facing to stitch the lining to.)

9. Turn the ribbon to the inside of the top and baste it down just below the seam between the ribbon and the fur.

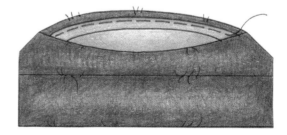

10. Add ½" around all four paper pattern pieces and cut out two body pieces and two sleeves from the satin lining fabric.

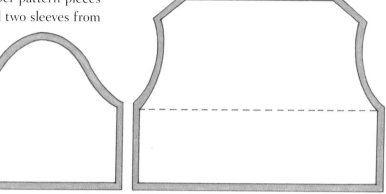

11. Using a ¾" seam allowance, sew the lining sides, shoulder seams, and sleeve seams together, back-tacking where you start and finish stitching. With the shoulder curve up and the wrist opening down, insert a sleeve into the body piece and pin it into the sleeve opening, matching the center top with the shoulder seams and the sleeve seams with the body side seams. Sew the sleeves into the sleeve openings. Press all of the seams open.

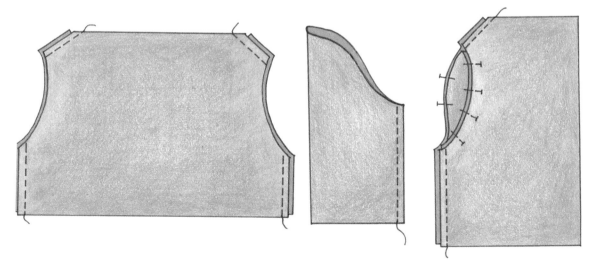

12. Place the lining inside the fur top, turn down the lining edge 1" to the wrong side of the lining, and pin the lining to the ribbon facing. Whipstitch the lining to the ribbon using a thread color to match the lining fabric.

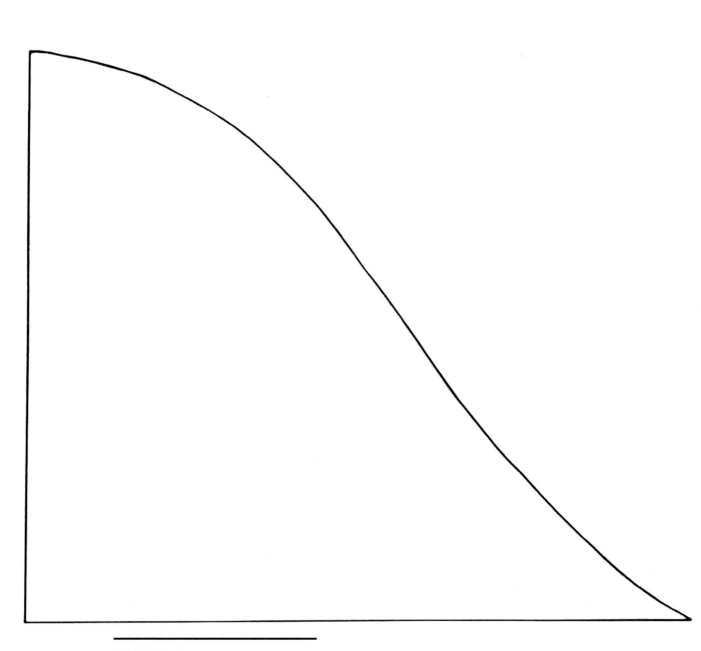

SLEEVE PATTERN
(shown at 100%)

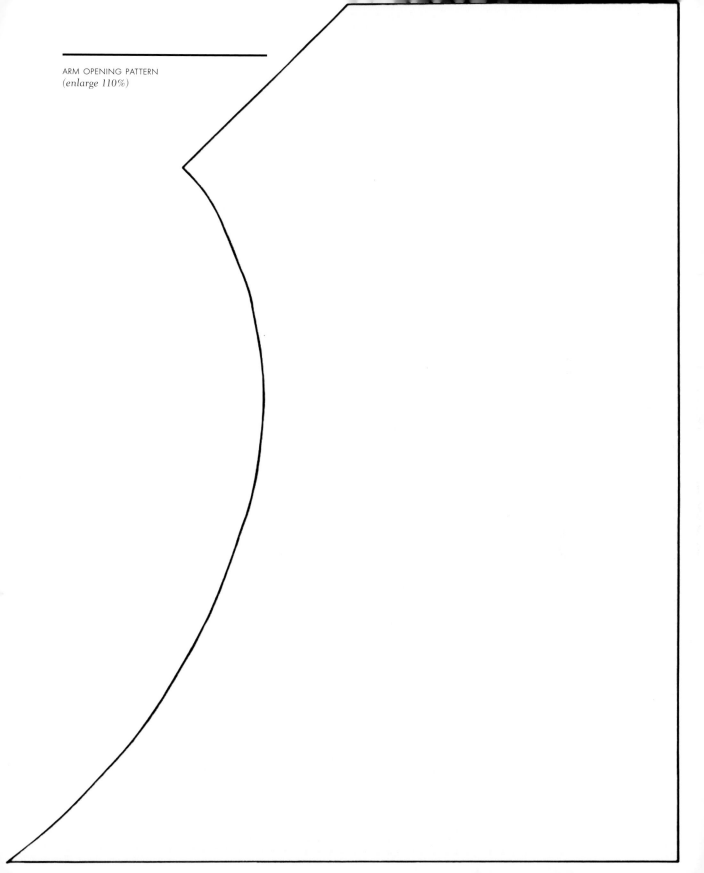

ARM OPENING PATTERN
(enlarge 110%)

FEATHERED EVENING CLUTCH

This project and the one that follows are great introductions to the world of working with feathers. The scale is not too overwhelming, but the impact certainly is. Any little black dress would happily be paired with either of these exuberant evening bags. I have included a few hot-fix rhinestones for added sparkle, but whether or not to include them is up to you, because really, a flock of chartreuse feathers is certainly enough glamour for one bag.

MATERIALS

¾ yard satin fabric

¾ heavy-weight fusible interfacing

½ yard ostrich feather

Hot-fix rhinestones (optional)

All-purpose thread to match fabric

TOOLS

Sewing machine

Iron

Pins

Hand-sewing needle

Tailor's chalk

MAKING THE FEATHERED
EVENING CLUTCH

1. Cut two 12" × 12" pieces and two 7" × 12" pieces from the satin. Cut one 12" × 12" piece and one 7" × 12" piece from the interfacing.

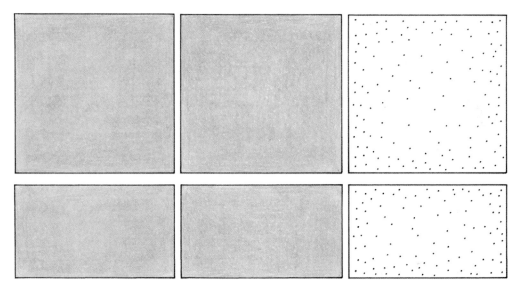

2. Fuse the interfacing to the wrong side of one 12" × 12" piece of satin and one 7" × 12" piece of satin. These will form the lining pieces.

3. With right sides together, sew the 7" × 12" pieces of satin together along one 12" edge. Turn the fabric right side out and press. This forms the bag front.

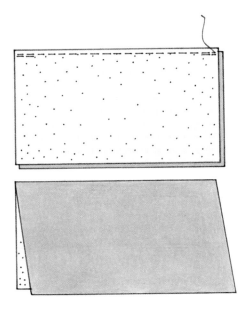

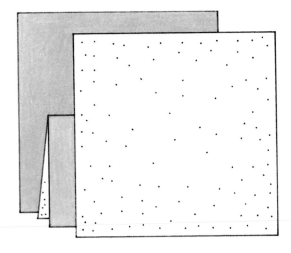

4. Layer the bag pieces in this order: the inter-faced 12" × 12" piece right side up, the bag front, and the 12" × 12" non-interfaced piece right side down. Make sure the raw edges of the bag front are aligned with the raw edges of the other pieces.

5. Pin all of the layers together and sew around all of the edges, leaving a 4" opening at the center top.

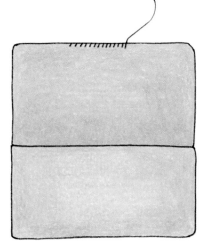

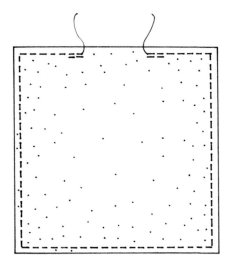

6. Turn the bag right side out through the opening in the flap. At the opening, fold under the raw edges and whip stitch the opening closed.

7. To form the bottom of the purse, turn the bag inside out, open up one corner, and line up the bottom and side seams to form a triangle. Mark a point ½" from the tip of the triangle. Sew across that point, perpendicular to the seam.

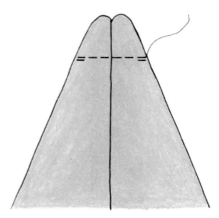

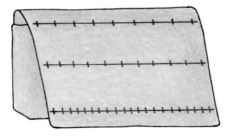

8. Measure 1" up from the bottom of the flap and use chalk to draw a line parallel to the flap's edge. Make chalk marks ⅜" apart along this line. Draw another line 2¾" from the edge of the flap. Draw marks 1" apart along this line. Draw the last line 4¾" up from the edge of the flap. Draw marks 1¾" apart along this line.

9. Tie 40 ostrich feather bundles. (See Working with Feathers on page 14.) Thread a needle using the long thread trailing from one of the feather bundles. Beginning at the bottom left, insert the needle though the outer layer of the flap fabric and bring it up just on the other side of the bundle. Repeat this stitch several times, then secure the thread and trim. Repeat until you have attached a feather bundle at each chalk mark, working across the bottom row before you move up to the next row.

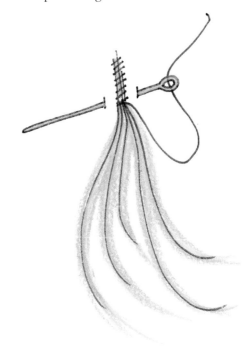

FEATHERED FRAME BAG

This version of the feathered bag requires a purchased bag frame, and the size of that frame will determine the size of the finished bag. My example uses a 7" frame, but the instructions will let you create a pattern based on any size frame you choose. Likewise, the amounts of fabric and batting called for here are for a 7" frame, but if your frame is substantially larger or smaller than that, you may need more or less. My advice is to create your pattern from your purse frame before you buy fabric. That way, you can measure the pieces before you shop and not find yourself with too much—or too little—fabric when it's time to start sewing.

MATERIALS

½ yard satin fabric

7" purse frame

½ yard quilt batting

¾ yard ostrich feather

Hot-fix rhinestones (optional)

All-purpose thread

Clear-drying craft glue

TOOLS

Sewing machine

Ruler

Scissors

Pins

Hand-sewing needle

Iron

Tailor's chalk

MAKING THE FEATHERED FRAME BAG

1. To make your pattern, take your frame and trace around the outside, including the points where the hinges stop.

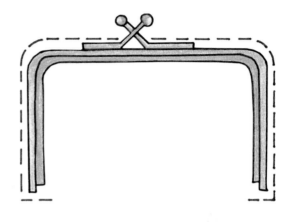

2. Draw a line ½" above the top of the traced frame. This line should begin ½" to the left of the traced frame and extend ½" past the traced frame. Flip the frame down and draw a line across the bottom, ½" away from the edge of the frame. This line should begin 3" to the left of the frame and extend 3" past the frame. Form a trapezoid by drawing two lines connecting the top and bottom lines. This forms the Purse Body Pattern (below).

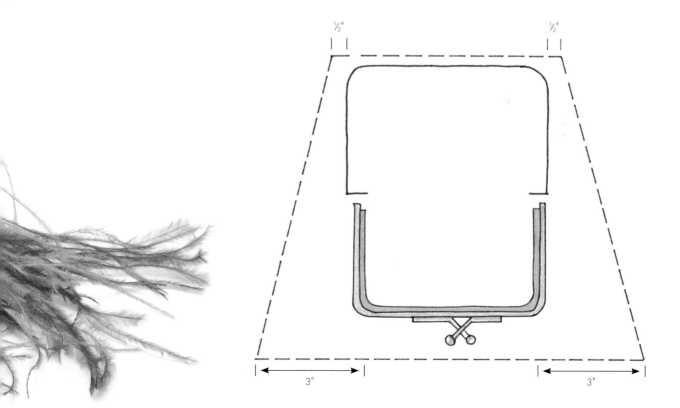

3. Using the pattern you just created and a sharp pair of scissors, cut four pieces from the satin and two pieces from the batting. Use pins to mark the hinge placement on both sides of the satin pieces.

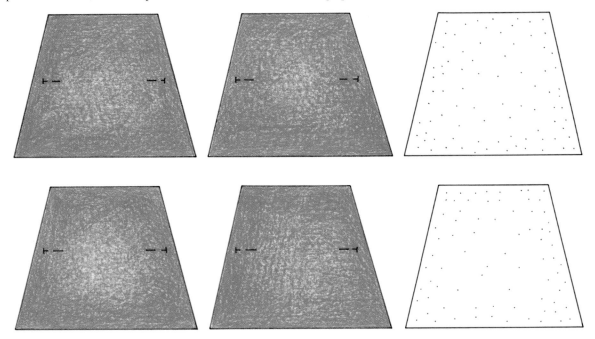

4. Layer a piece of batting, two satin pieces with right sides together, and another piece of batting. Pin the layers together. Starting at one pin marking the placement of the frame hinge, sew the sides and bottom of your bag, finishing at the hinge marking opposite where you started. Back-tack where you start and finish stitching.

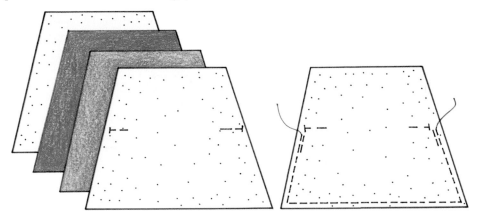

5. To create a flat bottom for your purse, open and flatten one of the corners of your bag, lining up the side seam with the bottom seam to form a triangle. Measure 1" from the tip of the triangle and mark that spot with a pin. Stitch across this mark per-pendicular to the seam line, back-tacking where you start and finish stitching. Trim the excess fabric ¼" from the seam. Repeat for the other bottom corner of the bag. Turn the bag right side out.

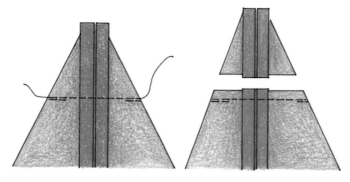

6. With right sides facing, pin the two remaining pieces of satin together. Mark the flap opening and hinge on the lining to match the mark you made on the exterior bag. Starting at one hinge, sew the lining, leaving a 4" gap in the bottom line of stitching and back-tacking where you start and finish stitching.

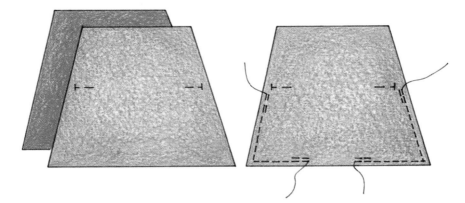

7. Create a flat bottom in the lining by opening and flattening one of the corners, lining up the side seam with the bottom seam to form a triangle. Measure 1" from the tip of the triangle and mark that spot with a pin. Stitch across this mark per-pendicular to the seam line, back-tacking where you start and finish stitching. Trim the excess fabric ¼" from the seam. Repeat for the other bottom corner of the lining.

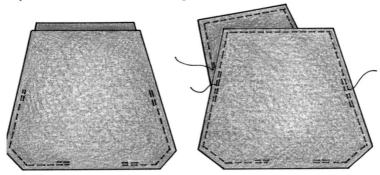

8. Slip the exterior bag (right side out) into the lining bag (wrong side out). The right sides of the bags should now be facing each other. On one of the flaps, pin the lining to the exterior bag at the top and sides. Begin sewing where the stitching starts on the lining, sew all around the flap, and stop at the stitching on the opposite side of the lining. Repeat with the other purse flap.

9. Pull the exterior bag through the hole in the stitching at the bottom of the lining. Whipstitch the opening in the lining closed. Push the lining into the exterior bag and smooth everything down, pressing with a press cloth from the outside, if

10. Apply glue to the channel on one side of the frame, starting at one hinge and working your way to the other. Insert the sides of your purse into the frame, starting at one hinge and working your way up to the top corner. Use a sharp object to poke and stuff the fabric evenly into the frame—small sewing scissors are perfect for this job. Repeat with the other side of that flap, again starting at the hinge. After you have inserted the sides of the purse into the frame, insert the top edge of the purse into the frame. Turn the purse over to check that the lining side is also inserted evenly into the frame. Let the glue dry for 15 minutes before tackling the other side of the frame in the same way.

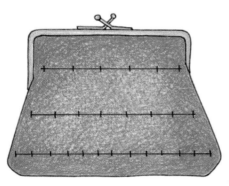

11. On both sides of the bag, measure 1" up from the crease that forms the bottom front edge, and draw a chalk line parallel to this crease. Make chalk marks ⅜" apart along this line. Draw another line 2¾" up from the crease. Draw marks 1" apart along this line. Draw the last line 4¼" up from the crease, and make marks 1¼" apart along this line.

12. Tie 52 ostrich feather bundles. (See Working with Feathers on page 14.) Thread a needle using the long thread trailing from one of the feather bundles. Beginning at the bottom left, insert the needle though the outer layer of the flap fabric and bring it up just on the other side of the bundle. Repeat this stitch several times, then secure the thread and trim. Repeat until you have attached a feather bundle at each chalk mark, working across the entire bottom of the bag before you move up to the next row. If desired, add a sprinkling of hot-fix rhinestones using a hot fixer.

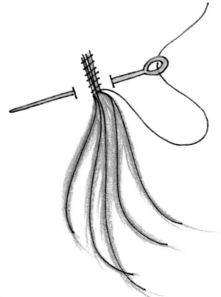

BRA NIGHTGOWN

I see any event in my life as a fashion moment. Delivering a baby is certainly an event, so when I was ready to give birth to my third, fourth, or fifth child (who's counting?), I went shopping for a nightgown to wear in the hospital. Surprisingly, there was nothing out there for me. The gowns I found were either too tight-fitting (not ideal when you are 9 months pregnant), too short, too sheer, or too bridal. There were loose-fitting gowns in flannel and cotton, but I was looking for something more Zsa Zsa Gabor than Laura Ingalls Wilder. As in so many other instances in my life, I decided to make my own. This project is so easy it's almost insulting, but the results are spectacular and the possibilities are endless. You can use a plain bra or a fancy one, a modest or a sexy one. Your gown can be long or short, sheer or opaque. This nightgown is quick to put together, so it makes a perfect last-minute gift. Make one up in white for a bridal shower gift, or make a sweet one in cotton for the girl on her way to college. Just don't get yourself in trouble by underestimating someone's bra size!

MATERIALS

¾ to 1½ yards
   (depending on the length
   you want your gown)
   60"-wide fabric

1 bra

All-purpose thread

TOOLS

Sewing machine

Pins

Hand-sewing needle

Flexible tape measure

MAKING THE BRA NIGHTGOWN

1. Fold your fabric in half so the selvage edges meet, with right sides together. Starting 8" from the top edge, sew a seam with a ½" seam allowance, back-tacking where you start and finish stitching. Press the seam open flat.

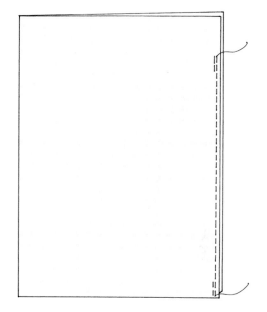

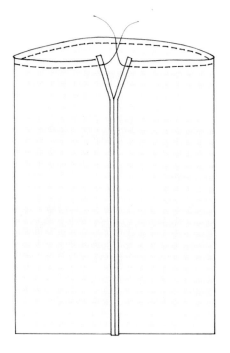

2. By hand or by machine, baste a row of stitching ½" from the edge.

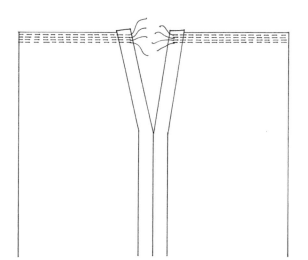

3. Baste another row of stitching ⅛" above the first row. Repeat twice more, for a total of four rows of basting, each ⅛" apart. The last row should be ⅛" from the raw edge of the fabric.

4. Put on the bra and measure around the bottom edge. (If you're making this for someone else, you'll need some assistance stretching out the band and taking this measurement.) This measurement will indicate how much you need to gather your basting stitches.

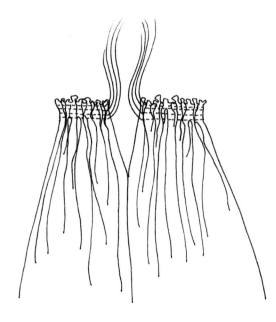

5. If the rows were basted by machine, gather the four top threads on one side and tie them together. Gather and tie together the four bobbin threads from the same side. Grasping the four bobbin threads from the other side, gently pull and gather the fabric until the opening matches the measurement you got in step 4 and the fabric is gathered evenly all the way around. If you basted by hand, there will be only four threads to tie together and four threads to pull.

6. Place the gathered fabric on a flat surface with the seam side down and the seam centered. Mark the center front, directly opposite the seam, with a pin. Keeping the fabric flat and the center front lined up with the back seam, mark each side with a pin.

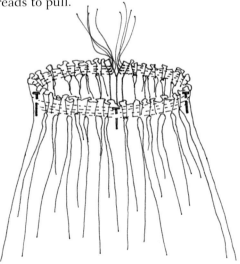

7. Pin the gathered fabric to the bra, matching the center front, sides, and back. Because the bra stretches when it is put on, the gathered fabric will be larger than the relaxed bra.

8. Starting at the back, stretch each section of the bra to fit the section of gathered fabric. Add some pins to hold each section in place. Whipstitch it by hand to the underside of the bra.

9. Hem the gown to the desired length by hand or machine.

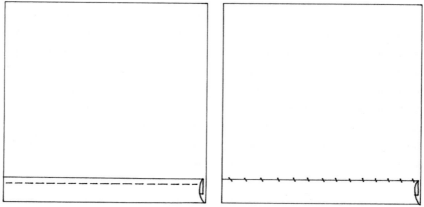

FURRY SLIPPERS

Admittedly, these slippers are a bit silly, highly impractical, and not exactly an item of high fashion. But they are luxurious, and they're not only easy to make, but they're also a great gift and a great conversation piece. Most importantly, they take just a small amount of fur to make, so they are a great way to use up all of the fur scraps you have left over from the other fur projects. When you make these, you are recycling recycled fur.

The pattern provided is for a medium slipper, about a women's size 7 or 8. You can adjust the size by lengthening or shortening the pattern in the area indicated. I reused the velvet lining from my fur stole for the main fabric and used silk satin for the contrasting fabric. The directions call for a thick piece of plastic (from a plastic folder) to add structure to the slipper. You can substitute a thin piece of cardboard, about the thickness of a cereal box, for the plastic.

MATERIALS

¼ yard fabric

¼ yard quilt batting

Plastic folder

Mink fur (1 square foot)

½ yard contrasting piping fabric

All-purpose thread

TOOLS

Sewing machine

Sharp scissors or snap blade cutter

Self-healing cutting mat

Pins

Hand-sewing needle

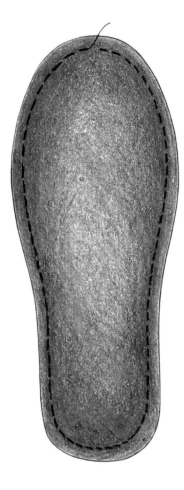

MAKING THE FURRY SLIPPERS

1. Using the Slipper Bottom Pattern (see page 196), cut four pieces out of fabric, two pieces out of quilt batting, and two pieces out of the plastic folder. Trim ¼" from the edge of the plastic pieces. Pin the slipper bottom pieces together in this order: fabric (right side down), plastic, batting, fabric (right side up). Sew around the edge of the slipper bottom using a ¼" seam allowance. Trim the seam allowance to ⅛". Repeat with the second slipper.

2. Use the Slipper Top Pattern (see page 197) to cut two pieces out of fabric and two pieces out of fur. With right sides facing, pin a piece of fabric and a piece of fur together and sew along the straight edge using a ¼" seam allowance. Repeat with the second set.

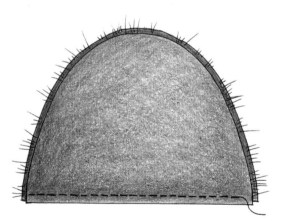

3. Turn one of the slipper tops right side out and use a hand-sewing needle and thread to baste along the curved edge. Repeat with the second slipper top.

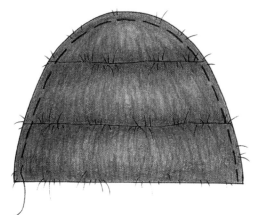

4. Pin a slipper top to a slipper bottom using the arrows and centerline as guides. Stitch the top and bottom together using a ¼" seam allowance. Back-tack where you start and finish stitching. Trim the fur to ⅛" from the stitching.

5. Cut two 1½" × 28" strips on the bias out of the piping fabric. With the right side down, pin a fabric strip to a slipper, overlapping the ends of the fabric by ½". Trim the excess strip away and repeat with the other strip and slipper.

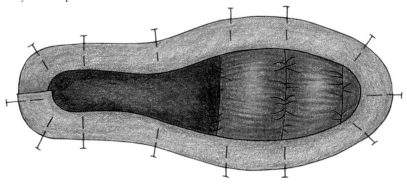

6. Stitch the bias strips to the slippers using a ¼"
seam allowance.

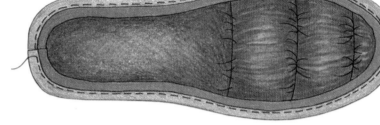

7. Fold the edge of one bias strip back to the
stitching line and turn the folded strip to the bottom of the slipper.

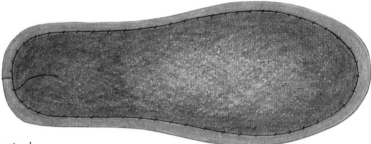

8. Whipstitch in place by hand. Repeat with the
second slipper.

9. Add a flourish such as a bow, and enjoy!

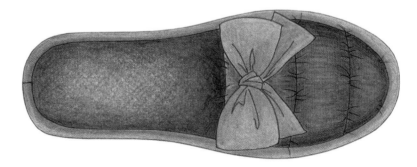

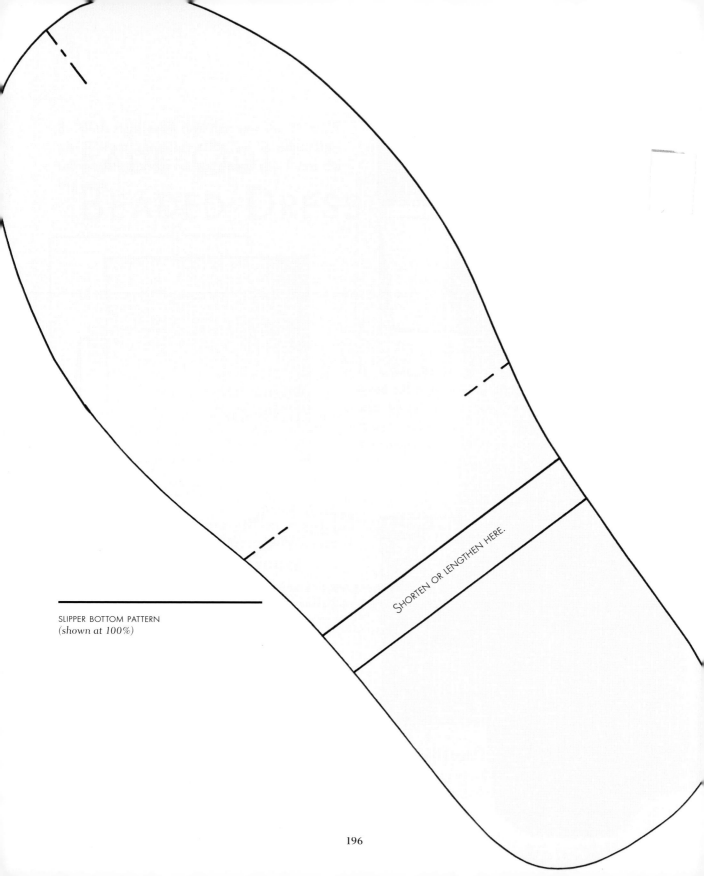

SLIPPER BOTTOM PATTERN
(shown at 100%)

SHORTEN OR LENGTHEN HERE.

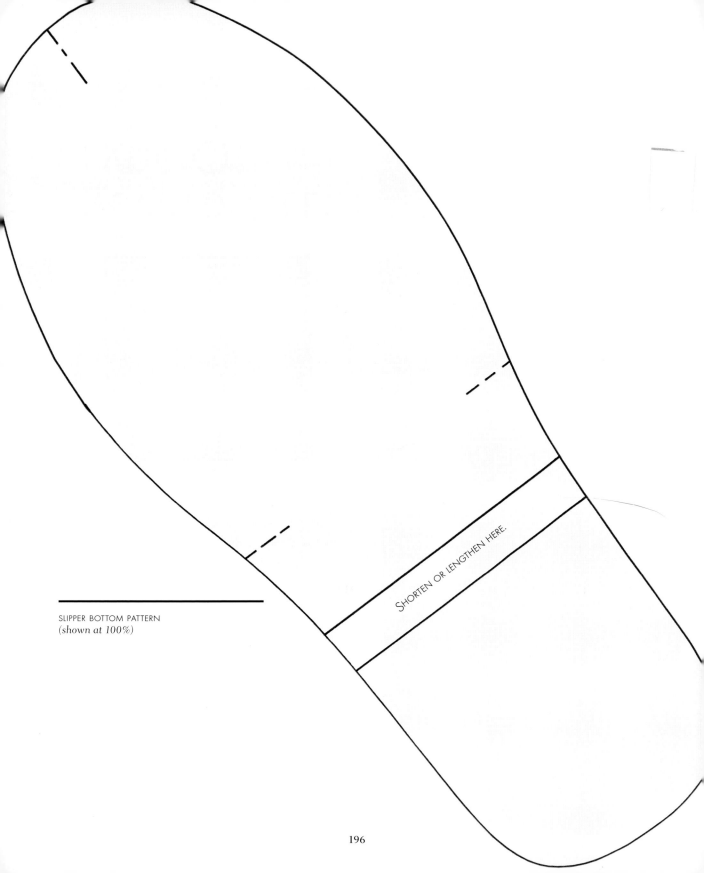

SLIPPER BOTTOM PATTERN
(shown at 100%)

SHORTEN OR LENGTHEN HERE.

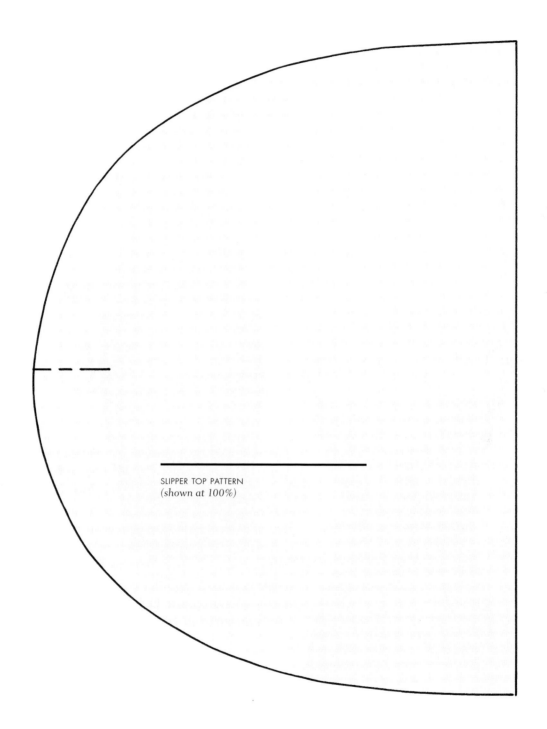

SLIPPER TOP PATTERN
(shown at 100%)

Acknowledgments

As with any creative project, this book is the collaboration of so many people, and I can't thank them enough.

First up was the team at Kuhn Projects, especially David Kuhn and Jessi Cimafonte, who worked so hard on putting the idea together. Next, the team at Rodale stepped in. Pam Krauss gave all the projects her sharp eye and saw exactly what was missing and what there was too much of (pink and green!). Victoria Glerum was given the thankless task of keeping me on schedule and she probably learned a lot more than she wanted to about sewing leather. Kara Plikaitis had to put up with my "input" on the layout design, and unnamed editors meticulously checked my instructions. They each did a phenomenal job.

Constance Hansen, Russell Peacock, and Edward Smith all did an amazing job at helping to develop the visual content through photography. My friends Susan Mercandetti, Marina Killery, M. K. Brinson, and Rachel Feder kept me connected, kept me inspired, and kept me going. I would also like to thank my Mom, for teaching me how to sew so many years ago.

But most of all, I thank my husband, Peter, whose constant help and encouragement makes it possible for me to do everything I do. As surrounded as I am by loving and creative people, life would be lonely without you.

Resources

Mink Stoles and Coats
www.ebay.com

FAUX FUR

Tissavel Faux Mink Fur
www.prefurs.com

Elegant Fabrics
222 West 40th Street
New York, NY 10018
212.302.4980

LEATHER

The Leather Guy
www.theleatherguy.org

Globalleather.com
253 West 35th Street, 9th Floor
New York, NY 10001
212.244.5190

Tandy Leather
www.tandyleatherfactory.com

iPhone and iPad, Kindle Clear Flexible Skin
www.amazon.com

3M 465 Adhesive Transfer Tape
www.drillspot.com

FABRIC, TRIM, ELASTIC

Mood Fabrics
225 West 37th Street
New York, NY 10018
212.730.5003

Elegant Fabrics
222 West 40th Street
New York, NY 10018
212.302.4980

HOT FIX RHINESTONES, BEADS, AND SEQUINS

M&J Trimmings
1008 6th Avenue
New York, NY 10018
212.391.6200
www.mjtrim.com

Joyce Trimming
109 West 38th Street
New York, NY 10018
212.719.3110
www.ejoyce.com

PURSE HARDWARE AND HANDLES

Hardware Elf
www.hardwareelf.com

Purse Supplies R Us
http://stores.ebay.com/ID-and-Purse-Supplies-R-Us

Joyce Trimming
109 West 38th Street
New York, NY 10018
212.719.3110
www.ejoyce.com

FEATHERS

The Feather Place
40 West 38th Street
New York, NY 10018
212.921.4452

M&J Trimmings
1008 6th Avenue
New York, NY 10018
212.391.6200
www.mjtrim.com

INDEX

Boldface page references indicate illustrations and photographs.